A Ray of Hope Series A10

PLURALISM WITH PURPOSE

Understanding Anekanta

MANDAN

BlueRose ONE.com
Stories Matter
NewDelhi • London

BLUEROSE PUBLISHERS

India | U.K.

BLUEROSE PUBLISHERS

www.BlueRoseONE.com

info@bluerosepublishers.com

+91 8882 898 898

+4407342408967

ISBN: 978-93-7310-621-2

JSBN: ARHMP0003

Book Name:

Pluralism with Purpose: Understanding Anekanta

Author:

Mandan (Shri Trailokyamandan Vijay Maharaj, A Jain Monk)

Publisher:

BlueRose Publishers

Series:

A Ray of Hope Series A10

Second Edition:

Veer 2551   A.D. 2025

Sponsor:

Arihant Park Jain Sangh, Surat

Contributor:

Shrut Premi Shravak Varg

Contact:

arayofhope.tm@gmail.com +91 83203 68605 &
mandanparivar2023@gmail.com +91 78620 07078

Introduction

- *Mandan*

In the midst of a world increasingly fragmented by ideological extremism, rigid opinions, and identity-driven conflicts, the need for balanced, inclusive thinking has never been more urgent. **Pluralism with Purpose: Understanding Anekanta** is an invitation to rediscover a timeless solution hidden in ancient Jain wisdom: Anekanta, the doctrine of manifold perspectives. This booklet is not just a study of a philosophical concept — it is a call to adopt a way of thinking that fosters harmony, tolerance, and truthful inquiry.

The core principle of Anekanta teaches that truth is multifaceted. No single statement, belief, or viewpoint can capture the complete truth on its own. Just as a single ray of light cannot reveal the entire form of an object, one perspective cannot fully comprehend the complexity of reality. Truth must be approached through multiple lenses, recognizing the partial validity in each and transcending the temptation to absolutize any one of them.

The purpose of this booklet is to make Anekanta approachable and practical. Through a series of structured discourses, simplified explanations, everyday illustrations, and reflective exercises, readers are encouraged not only to understand Anekanta intellectually, but to live it experientially. Whether you are a student, a teacher, a spiritual seeker, or simply someone curious about the Jain path of wisdom, this booklet offers tools to cultivate a mind that is open, balanced, and rooted in deeper understanding.

Each discourse in **Pluralism with Purpose: Understanding Anekanta** is designed to address a specific dimension of pluralistic thinking — ranging from the metaphysical triad of Dravya, Guna, and Paryaya to the practical application of Syadvad, Nayavad, and the concept of Saptabhangi. The text is supported by reflection questions and short practices to help you internalize and apply the teachings in day-to-day decision-making, relationships, and spiritual practice.

The intended audience for this booklet is wide and inclusive. It is written in simple yet precise language to benefit both beginners and serious students of Jain thought. Young readers will find clarity; mature readers will discover depth. Educators may use it as a teaching tool, and spiritual aspirants may find it a trustworthy companion on the path of self-realization.

Understanding and practicing Anekanta is no longer a philosophical luxury — it has become a moral necessity. In today's world, where differences of opinion often breed hatred, where disagreement is mistaken for enmity, and where truth is used more as a weapon than a guide, Anekanta teaches us to embrace nuance, respect others' journeys, and seek clarity rather than victory. It is a philosophy that replaces judgment with inquiry, arrogance with humility, and chaos with equanimity.

Furthermore, Anekanta serves as a bridge between spiritual wisdom and ethical living. It teaches us that true non-violence (Ahinsa) is not just refraining from harm in action, but also in thought and speech. When we accept the possibility that another person may be partially right, we disarm our ego and open the door to peaceful coexistence. In this way, Anekanta becomes the silent strength of Jain philosophy — the invisible pillar holding up the vast edifice of truth.

May **Pluralism with Purpose: Understanding Anekanta** guides you toward a more thoughtful, compassionate, and truthful way of living. Let this humble offering serve as a stepping stone on your journey toward spiritual clarity, inner balance, and the ultimate goal — Moksha, liberation of the soul through right knowledge, right faith, and right conduct.

About the Series

A Ray of Hope is more than a name — it's a quiet promise. A promise to share wisdom that heals, awakens, and uplifts.

Rooted in the timeless principles of Jain philosophy, yet deeply relevant to the modern soul, A Ray of Hope A – Adhyayan Series is an initiative to enlighten the youth with the eternal teachings of Tirthankar Mahavira. our mission is to create books, content, and experiences that inspire inner clarity and spiritual courage, while bringing his profound wisdom into everyday life.

We believe that every soul holds a silent strength — waiting to be remembered. Our work is to reignite that remembrance — not through rigid preaching, but through stories, questions, and metaphors that speak directly to the heart.

We write for the youth. For seekers who want depth without heaviness, tradition without dogma, and truth that can be lived — not just quoted.

Each book we create is crafted with care, reflection, and reverence — so that it doesn't just teach, but *touches*.

To stay connected or explore more:

Mobile: +91 83203 68605

Email: arayofhope.tm@gmail.com

Instagram: @arayofhope_arh

Website: www.mandanparivar.com

Part One

DISCOURSES ON ANEKANTA

Part 1 – Discourses on Anekanta

Index

Image description

This image powerfully illustrates the concept of Anekanta, where opposites coexist in harmony. The meditating figure at the centre symbolizcs thc balanccd soul, rooted in awareness amidst dual realities. One side reflects the scientific, logical world: the other, spiritual depth and intuitive truth. Anekanta teaches us that both perspectives — material and spiritual — are valid and necessary. Just as light rcvcals different colours through different angles, truth unfolds through many viewpoints. This image captures the unity within diversity, the essence of Anekanta.

Discourse 01

ANEKANTA: THE SILENT STRENGTH OF JAIN PHILOSOPHY

Introduction:

In a world increasingly divided by beliefs, opinions, and perspectives, Jain philosophy offers a timeless principle that can heal conflicts both within and outside us — Anekanta.

Rooted in the vision of Tirthankar Mahavira, Anekanta teaches us that truth is never one-dimensional. This article explores the philosophical depth of Anekanta, the misconceptions around Syadvad, and how this ancient idea remains more relevant than ever — not just as a spiritual principle, but as a way of life.

Key theme:

This discourse introduces Anekanta as the foundational vision of Jain philosophy — the art of perceiving reality through multiple perspectives. In a world divided by rigid opinions, Anekanta encourages open-mindedness, spiritual maturity, and balanced understanding. It is not just a doctrine but a guide for resolving internal and external conflicts.

Understanding the Wisdom Beyond One-Sidedness

Any philosophy has a central vision of its own, based on which the philosophy stands. For example, Buddhists have a vision of Ephemerality (impermanence). They believe that everything is momentary. Buddhist philosophy emerged based on this belief. Then there is Vedanta, whose central vision is of Maya (illusion). The whole world is an illusion; Brahma is the truth. The entire philosophy of Vedanta stems from the principle of Maya (illusion). Similarly, The foundation of Jain philosophy rests on Pluralism (Anekanta). All the ideologies of the Jain philosophy are based on Anekanta.

What is Ekanta (one-sidedness)?

In this context, 'anta' means an opinion formed after thorough consideration of all parameters.

A view that is still under contemplation — not yet finalized — cannot be termed an opinion. Only when a decision is made does it become an 'anta' (opinion).

An opinion formed by considering only one aspect while rejecting all other possibilities is called Ekanta (one-sidedness).

In simple terms, a conclusion drawn from just one perspective, without acknowledging other viewpoints, is Ekanta.

Conversely, Anekanta (Pluralism) means refraining from clinging to a single point of view. It involves exploring all possible perspectives and striving to grasp the whole truth.

An opinion that arises after contemplating multiple viewpoints is known as Anekanta.

The complete truth revealed through this multi-angled thinking is the essence of Anekanta.

When Anekanta is applied to various objects and situations, it manifests differently — sometimes referred to as Syadvad, sometimes as Nayavad, sometimes as Panchakaran-samavay, and other times as *Utpad-Vyaya-Dhrauvya.*

Thus, Syadvad and Nayavad are specific methods of expressing Anekanta, but they are not synonymous with Anekanta itself.

In short, Syadvad is a part of Anekanta — a means of expressing it — not Anekanta in its entirety. The words, phrases, and sentences crafted to present Anekanta to the world are categorized as Syadvad, Nayavad, Tripadi, and so on.

Anekanta: Acceptance of Contradictory Properties

The true acceptance of contradictory properties within a single entity is the heart of Anekanta.

For instance:

You are a son from your father's point of view and a father from your son's point of view.

Can a single person be both son and father?

If someone answers — "One can either be a son or a father" — that is Ekanta (one-sidedness).

However, acknowledging that from one perspective he is a son, and from another he is a father is Anekanta.

Here, two seemingly contradictory identities — sonhood and fatherhood — coexist within the same person, depending on the perspective adopted.

If you insist that a person must either be only a father or only a son, you fall into Ekanta.

But if you change your viewpoint according to the context, you realize the truth of both aspects together — and that is the beauty of Anekanta.

The Behaviour of the World is attributed to Anekanta

Shri Siddhasen Diwakarji states in the *Sanmati-tarka* (an important Jain scripture) that no actions in the world happen without Anekanta.

The entire world operates by adopting multiple perspectives, knowingly or unknowingly.

However, when it comes to applying Anekanta in the realm of philosophy or spiritual thought, people often hesitate.

In everyday life, we naturally accept plurality – for instance, we easily recognize that a person can simultaneously be someone's daughter and someone else's mother.

Thus, we are already living in plurality.

Yet, because we are not consciously analysing or reflecting on it, we fail to truly understand Anekanta.

Anekanta in Practical Life: Light and Darkness

To explain this more practically – Suppose I ask you: "Is there light or darkness in this hall?"

If you wish to give a realistic answer, you would say: "There is light here, but there is darkness in that corner."

This is an example of Anekanta — the acceptance that both light and darkness exist within the same hall, depending on the perspective.

Thus, whenever we view a situation from multiple angles and recognize differing realities based on context, we are practising Anekanta.

Anekanta: The Ability to Hold Contradictions

The most powerful definition of Anekanta is: "The ability to hold multiple, even contradictory, properties within the same entity depending on the perspective."

At first glance, when someone says: "There is both darkness and light in this hall," it may seem absurd. But when we understand the role of perspectives, we realize that both statements can be true.

Thus, Anekanta teaches us to rise above one-dimensional thinking.

Why the World Has Misunderstood Anekanta

Throughout history, many philosophies — starting from Vedanta and others — have rejected Anekanta. They failed to grasp its subtle yet expansive essence.

Diwakarji Bhagwant rightly states that no ordinary action in life happens without some degree of Anekanta.

For example, if I ask you right now: "Are you wearing clothes or not?"

From one perspective, you are wearing clothes — your body is covered. From another, your face, hands, or parts of your body may be uncovered. Thus, you are both wearing clothes and not wearing clothes, depending on the viewpoint.

This simple example shows how Anekanta operates naturally in life, but because we don't consciously reflect on it, we miss its deeper philosophical significance.

The Mission of Anekanta: Opening Perspectives

The core purpose of Anekanta is to expand our vision — to open our minds to multiple dimensions of reality.

Most people, stuck in narrow viewpoints, develop conflicts — within themselves, with others, in society, religion, and even at the national level. Because they fail to understand the context or the perspective from which another person is speaking, disputes arise.

Thus, the greatest contribution of Anekanta is to encourage understanding, tolerance, and depth: To see the underlying reasons, contexts, and truths behind every viewpoint.

The Tragedy: Misunderstanding Anekanta

While the Jain philosophy stands firmly on the foundation of Anekanta, it is unfortunate that many Jains themselves have not fully understood even the "A" of Anekanta.

Tirthankar Mahavira had reached the pinnacle of both thought and conduct. He bestowed upon humanity two unparalleled gifts:

Anekanta at the level of thought.

Ahinsa (non-violence) at the level of conduct.

Yet today, while many strive to practise non-violence externally through rituals, few grasp the depth of non-violence in thought, which is embodied in Anekanta.

Difference Between Jain Philosophy and Jain Religion

Philosophy is the study and understanding of fundamental questions about life.

It emerges from humanity's innate curiosity — a curiosity that sets humans apart from all other living beings.

Animals, for instance, live in the jungle without ever wondering: "How big is this jungle?" or "What is the name of this jungle?" Such questions arise only in humans because of their deep-seated urge to seek truth.

As humans evolve, their curiosity grows. They begin asking profound questions — not just about daily survival but about life itself:

- Who am I?
- Where did I come from?
- Where am I destined to go?
- What is the purpose of my life?
- Is there something better beyond the life I am living?
- What causes my happiness and my suffering?
- If something causes happiness, can it be increased?
- If something causes suffering, can it be reduced?
- Is there a way to transcend the cycle of happiness and sorrow?

Since time immemorial, humanity has wrestled with these timeless inquiries. Those rare individuals who succeeded in finding answers — through practice, experience, and realization — became revered as sages and saints.

The Birth of Darshan (Philosophical Systems)

When these enlightened beings shared their insights, their teachings gradually evolved into structured frameworks known as Darshan (philosophical systems). Darshan refers to an organized view of the Truth – a way of perceiving reality systematically.

In India alone, more than eighty major Darshans have been recognized historically, including:

- Jain Darshan (Jain Philosophy)
- Buddhist Darshan
- Charvaka Darshan
- Shaiva Darshan
- Vaisheshika Darshan
- Sankhya Darshan
- Mimamsa Darshan
- Vedanta Darshan
- Yoga Darshan and many others.

Despite their diversity, all Darshans share a common thread – they are human attempts to organize, interpret, and express the fundamental truths of existence.

The Unique Standpoint of Jain Philosophy

Among all these Darshans, Jain philosophy stands uniquely apart.

Most philosophies are built around defending their own principles while refuting others. However, Jain philosophy does not focus on rebuttal.

Instead, it seeks to harmonize truths from various perspectives, creating a dialogue among different philosophies.

The key that allows this harmonious dialogue is Pluralism (Anekantavad).

Jain philosophy endeavours to integrate the partial truths revealed by different traditions and to synthesize them toward a greater, more complete understanding — an Absolute Truth.

What Is Jain Religion?

While Jain Darshan refers to the philosophical understanding, Jain Religion is the practical application of that philosophy.

In simple terms:

- Philosophy = Knowledge and wisdom.
- Religion = Conduct and practice.

Thus, Jain philosophy provides the vision, and Jain religion provides the way of life to embody that vision.

At the heart of Jain philosophy is Anekanta (the acceptance of multiple truths), and at the heart of Jain religion is Ahinsa (non-violence).

The great masters have said:

"Anekanta, when lived through conduct, becomes Ahinsa; and Ahinsa, when lived through thought, becomes Anekanta."

Both Anekanta and Ahinsa share a common thread — tolerance. A truly tolerant soul:

- Listens to others' views calmly.
- Understands the deeper context.
- Responds thoughtfully and respectfully.

Reasons for Differences in Vision

To understand why differences in perspectives arise, consider this simple yet powerful analogy:

Imagine a mountain where six people are sitting at the top. Each of them views the same horizon, but their ability to see differs because of various factors:

- One person has a cataract that hasn't been treated.

- Another has undergone cataract surgery but has forgotten to wear glasses.
- The third wears glasses.
- The fourth has perfect vision without any aid.
- The fifth is a child with underdeveloped eyesight.
- The sixth is an elderly person whose vision has weakened with age.

Even though they all look at the same place, their experiences are different because:

- Their physical conditions differ.
- External factors like day or night, clear skies or clouds, also affect what they see.
- Internal factors like mental focus or physical health influence perception too.
- Thus, multiple layers — internal, external, physical, and psychological — affect vision.

The Deeper Meaning Behind This Analogy

The same principle applies in the realm of philosophy.

Different thinkers, though gazing at the same ultimate truth, perceive it differently based on their:

- Mental clarity,
- Spiritual maturity,
- Intellectual capacity,
- State of attachment or detachment,
- Depth of contemplation.

The problem arises when someone clings to their limited perception and believes that their understanding is the entire truth. Attachment to one's own partial experience creates conflict.

Anekantvad: The Epitome of Tolerance

If we examine the history of human conflict, five major reasons emerge: Land, Women, Wealth, Power, Religion.

Among these, the most devastating wars have been fought in the name of religion — far more than for any of the other causes combined. Why? Because while it is possible to give up desires for wealth, land, or power, it is far more difficult to give up attachment to one's own beliefs.

When religious attachment becomes rigid, it demands that everyone else must adopt the same belief.

This leads to violence, crusades, forced conversions, and wars.

The essence of these conflicts is not merely external struggle — it is internal stubbornness.

In Jain terminology, this stubbornness is called Ekanta (one-sidedness).

How Anekanta Breaks Stubbornness

Anekanta teaches us to act, but without attachment. Action with attachment is Ekanta. Action without attachment is Anekanta. We can hold an opinion, but we must not become attached to that opinion.

This is the core teaching of Anekanta — openness without clinging. Thus, non-violence (Ahinsa) governs conduct, and pluralism (Anekanta) governs thought.

Together, they create a life of love, compassion, wisdom, and true tolerance.

Non-Violence and Anekanta: Two Pillars of Spiritual Living

Ahinsa (Non-violence) governs conduct. Anekanta (Pluralism) governs thought.

Anekanta means striving to understand reality from multiple perspectives to uncover the truth. Non-violence means putting yourself in others' situations and responding with compassion, love, and understanding.

In Anekanta, we seek truth everywhere. In Non-violence, we seek the soul everywhere.

Thus:

- Anekanta is the search for multiple truths,
- Ahinsa is the search for the oneness of life.

Why Other Philosophies Could Not Accept Anekanta

A natural question arises: If Anekanta is such a profound principle, why didn't other philosophies adopt it? Why is it unique to Jainism? The answer lies in human nature.

To embrace Anekanta requires:

- Vastness of vision,
- Generosity of intention,
- Surrender of ego.

It demands hard work — the willingness to look beyond superficial truths toward the deeper reality. Most people find comfort in simple, one-dimensional explanations rather than in striving for the complete, complex truth.

Tirthankar Mahavira showed the path to self-realization, encouraging independent thinking.

In contrast, Goshalak, a contemporary ascetic teacher, prescribed easy practices without demanding deep understanding — hence, he attracted more followers.

Humans generally prefer:

- Simplicity over depth,
- Blind following over independent inquiry,
- Comfort over challenge.

Thus, Ekanta (one-sidedness) attracts the masses, while Anekanta draws only those willing to think, question, and expand their vision.

Ekanta: The Comfort of Certainty

Where there is Ekanta, people feel secure. It says: "This is the only way." "This alone is the truth."

Whereas Anekanta says: "This can also be this." "From another perspective, it can also be that."

Because Anekanta demands effort, openness, and tolerance, it often faces resistance.

The world has historically doubted Anekanta, misunderstood it, and sometimes even rejected it.

Divisiveness (Vibhajyavad): The Methodology Behind Anekanta

Anekanta is not just the acceptance of multiple truths – it begins with a method called Divisiveness (Vibhajyavad).

Tirthankar Mahavira taught that before answering any philosophical question, we must first break it down into its components.

Example 1:

- Question: "Are living beings better asleep or awake?"
- Response: "It depends: bad-minded are better asleep; good-natured are better awake."

Example 2:

- Question: "Can we eat Maas?" 'Maas' in Prakrit has two meanings – Meat and Black Lentil. Thus:
  - Meat: "No, it should not be eaten."
  - Black Lentil: "Yes, it can be eaten."

Breaking the question down reveals the correct context, leading to the right understanding.

This divisiveness — separating and analysing the layers of meaning — evolved into the larger philosophy of Anekanta.

The Basic Concept of Pluralism (Anekanta)

The essence of Anekanta is not to refute anyone's opinion — It is to refute the attachment behind the opinion.

No single opinion is entirely true or entirely false. Every viewpoint captures only a part of the truth.

Thus, Anekanta teaches:

- Respect all viewpoints,
- Correct the insistence and stubbornness that arises from partial understanding,
- Seek the fuller, more complete truth.

Pluralism: Acceptance of Relative Truth

Pluralism (Anekanta) tells us that:

All truths we perceive are relative truths — partial glimpses.

The Tirthankar emphasized the importance of recognizing relative knowledge. Whatever knowledge we hold is true only in a certain context, not in absolute terms.

Thus, a true seeker strives not to cling to any opinion but keeps striving toward higher understanding.

Practical Application of Anekanta

When we practise Anekanta, we sharpen our intellect and develop the ability to:

- Understand others' perspectives clearly,
- Grasp the underlying context and motivations,
- Reduce conflict through deeper comprehension.

Many conflicts — even among Jains — arise because, although people study Anekanta, they still cling to their own partial understanding, believing it to be the complete truth.

Mama Satyam: The Root of Conflict

In Sanskrit, the word for war is Mama Satyam, which literally means:

"The truth is only with me."

Whenever someone believes that their view alone is the complete truth, conflict becomes inevitable. Thus, wars — whether religious, ideological, or personal — often stem from attachment to one's limited viewpoint.

True Anekanta requires dissolving the ego attached to one's knowledge.

The Challenge of Accepting an Omniscient Being

Only one who can dissolve attachment to his own opinions can recognize an Omniscient Being as Omniscient. Even when people attended Tirthankar Mahavira's divine assembly (Samavasaran), not all accepted His words. Some came not to learn but to find fault.

Such individuals would often say: "What nonsense was being said!"

Yet, when questioned, they would have no clear explanation — only an emotional rejection, based on preconceived notions.

Thus, ego, not rational understanding, becomes the barrier to recognizing deeper truths.

Clarifying the Nature of Truth

Everything is true only from a certain perspective.

A thing cannot be universally true from all angles simultaneously. Misunderstanding a context and calling it "pluralism" is not real Anekanta — it is Mithya Anekanta (false pluralism).

True Anekanta demands:

- Sincerity in seeking,
- Humility in knowing,
- Non-attachment to one's opinions.

Anekanta: The Movement towards Absolute Truth

Any statement made with a clear explanation of its context can be called closer to absolute truth.

Because then, it implicitly acknowledges:

"From another context, this truth may change."

Tirthankar Mahavira, even during his spiritual discourses (Deshna), always clarified: "I speak from a specific viewpoint (Nay)." "This is the perspective from which I am answering."

This is the essence of Anekanta — the awareness that every truth has a context, and when the context changes, the truth may appear differently.

Understanding Mithyatva and Samyaktva through Anekanta

Let us now understand the difference between a Mithyatvi (one with wrong perception) and a Samyaktvi (one with right perception).

Suppose both are shown a pen.

- The Mithyatvi says: "This is a pen."
- The Samyaktvi also says: "This is a pen."

But there's a critical difference. The Mithyatvi is attached to this identity — unaware of its relativity. He believes the pen is an absolute entity — fixed and final.

The Samyaktvi, however, understands that:

- This pen is a temporary formation.
- It was something else in the past (e.g., metal).
- It will become something else in the future (e.g., scrap).
- Its current identity is contextual, valid only for the present moment.

Even if the Samyaktvi doesn't explain this each time, he is aware of the changing nature of all things. That subtle awareness comes from Anekanta and Syadvad.

Syadvad: The Heart of Jain Identity

Upadhyay Shri Yashovijayji has rightly said: "One who does not understand Syadvad is not a true Jain."

Why? Because without Syadvad – the structured application of Anekanta – one cannot grasp the absolute truth.

Even though the absolute truth cannot be fully spoken, a Syadvadi, when he speaks or thinks, always considers the context and limitations. Thus, his statements become relatively complete.

The Humility of the Samyaktvi

A Mithyatvi says: "I know." A Samyaktvi says: "Whatever I know is limited."

- The Mithyatvi creates boundaries around his understanding – he closes the door to new truths.
- The Samyaktvi remains open, knowing that all knowledge is subject to time, space, and perspective.

Because of this openness, the Samyaktvi can grow, evolve, and ultimately reach the absolute truth. Anekanta is the bridge that makes this journey possible.

Avoid Rushing to Judgment

In today's world, people are quick to form opinions — to judge without understanding.

Anekanta cautions us: "Don't sit on the judge's chair unless you're truly qualified."

Just as a judge must:

Know the law,

Understand past rulings,

Be neutral and unbiased,

Similarly, to form a fair opinion — or to call oneself a true Jain — one must:

1. Know the universal laws (like Karma, Syadvad, etc.),
2. Understand how the saints applied these principles,
3. Maintain neutrality — free from ego and emotion.

If even one of these is missing, you are not ready to form a conclusion — and in that case, the right path is to surrender the case, not give a verdict.

So too in life: If you have not yet reached the truth, don't form an opinion. Just keep seeking. That is Anekanta.

Anekanta: A Way of Seeing, A Way of Being

Anekanta is not just a concept to study — it is a vision to carry into every moment of life. It teaches us that no single view holds the whole truth, and no truth is complete without context.

To live Anekanta is to:

- Listen without the urge to refute,
- Speak with awareness of limitation,
- Think with openness and humility.

In a world quick to judge and slow to understand, Anekanta reminds us: real strength lies in holding space for many truths. It is not weakness to accept multiple viewpoints — it is wisdom.

May we learn to see as the Tirthankaras saw — not just with intellect, but with insight. Not just with certainty, but with compassion.

Anekanta is not the end of knowing. It is the beginning of true understanding.

Discourse 01

Reflection questions

1. How do I usually respond when someone challenges my beliefs? Do I react with curiosity or defensiveness?
2. In what situations have I applied the principles of Utsarg (the general rule) and Apavad (the exception) in my own actions or judgments?
3. Can I identify a recent moment where seeing multiple perspectives helped me avoid conflict or understand a situation better?

Discourse 01

Short practices

Philosophical:

Write about beliefs you held. Now, reframe them from another person's perspective. Reflect on how your understanding shifts when viewed from both lenses.

Journal:

Reflect on a recent disagreement. How could considering multiple perspectives have shifted your response?

Behavioural:

For one day, practice not interrupting anyone. Listen fully before responding.

Meditation:

Sit for 5 minutes, repeating the affirmation – 'There is truth in every viewpoint.'

Image description

This image beautifully reflects the spirit of Anekanta through its depiction of many individuals walking different paths toward the same radiant mountain peak. Each traveller represents a unique perspective, journey, or truth — yet all are moving toward the same ultimate goal. The varied landscapes and winding roads signify that truth can be approached from multiple directions. Anekanta teaches us to respect each path, knowing that the destination remains one — just understood differently. The glowing peak crowned with a lotus symbolizes enlightenment through multiplicity of viewpoints.

Discourse 02

ANEKANTA: THE SEARCH FOR ABSOLUTE TRUTH

Introduction:

The pursuit of truth is the aim of Anekanta. More precisely, it is the pursuit of absolute truth — not fragmented or partial truths, but a complete, contextual understanding. While partial truths may come to us naturally, seeking absolute truth requires conscious effort. Anekanta represents the fusion of completeness and authenticity, and the outcome of this fusion is the realization it strives for.

Key theme:

This discourse explores how Anekanta leads us from partial to absolute truth by overcoming internal limitations like ignorance, ego, and prejudice. It reveals the nine inner barriers that obstruct true perception and offers a path to transcend them. In practice, it inspires deep introspection and intellectual humility.

The Nature of Perception and Conflict

Anekanta teaches that every knowledgeable individual possesses varying degrees of:

- Intellect
- Information
- Understanding
- Experience
- Inner strength

When these five elements are combined, they create the foundation to grasp absolute truth. Since each person perceives truth differently, varied realizations emerge. These differences often become the root of conflict.

In early civilizations, conflicts were fewer — life was driven by basic survival. But as human intellect evolved, knowledge deepened, and with it came differences in perception. Anekanta emerged as an effort to resolve these conflicts of understanding.

Anekanta and the Barriers to Absolute Truth

According to the philosophy of Anekanta, the path to absolute truth is often obstructed by various inner limitations. While truth exists, our ability to perceive and accept it is hindered by nine significant barriers. Anekanta teaches that overcoming these internal obstacles is essential to truly grasp the essence of reality.

1. ***Ignorance***

   The most fundamental barrier is ignorance. When we lack understanding, truth naturally eludes us. Without knowledge or awareness, there is no foundation upon which truth can be realized.

2. ***Incorrect Knowledge***

   The second obstacle is possessing flawed or misconstrued knowledge. When our under-standing is built upon false assumptions, we are misled and unable to access the truth.

3. ***Prejudice***

   Preconceived notions and rigid thinking form the third barrier. When we approach situations with the belief that there is only one right way to think or act, we become closed to alternative perspectives, keeping truth out of reach.

4. ***Ego***

   Even when we recognize the truth, our ego may prevent us from accepting it. The need to be right or to protect our identity often overpowers the willingness to embrace what is correct.

5. ***Attachment***

We tend to cling to our current beliefs and opinions, convinced that our way is the only right way. This emotional attachment makes it difficult to consider or accept anything contrary.

6. ***Blind Selfishness***

Often, our self-interest clouds our judgment. Even when we know what is true, we may choose to ignore it because it doesn't serve our personal goals. A classic example is Dhritarashtra, who confessed to Krishna and Sanjay that he knew the Kauravas were wrong and the Pandavas were right. Yet, his bias and attachment prevented him from acknowledging the truth.

7. ***Lack of Wisdom***

A refusal to question or analyse reflects a lack of wisdom. Many people resist introspection, fearing it may lead to doubt or confusion. They prefer to accept things at face value, avoiding the effort required to distinguish truth from illusion.

8. ***Temptations***

Worldly desires often tempt us away from the truth. Accepting the truth may come at the cost of comfort, material gain, or social approval—leading many to turn a blind eye to what is right.

9. ***Intolerance***

   Perhaps the greatest barrier is intolerance. We often lack the patience to listen to differing viewpoints, let alone accept them. The moment someone challenges our beliefs; we react with anger or resistance instead of curiosity or contemplation.

In Summary:

To truly seek and accept the truth, Anekanta reminds us to rise above these nine barriers:

1. Ignorance
2. Incorrect Knowledge
3. Prejudice
4. Ego
5. Attachment
6. Blind Selfishness
7. Lack of Wisdom
8. Temptations
9. Intolerance

The path to absolute truth requires an open mind, self-awareness, and the courage to let go of what holds us back. Anekanta is not merely about seeing multiple perspectives – it is about nurturing the inner clarity and humility necessary to receive the truth in its purest form.

Anekanta: The Path to Overcoming Inner Obstacles

The key to overcoming the nine barriers that obstruct our path to absolute truth lies in the principle of Anekanta. When Anekanta becomes an active part of our thinking and living, transformation begins from within.

First, ignorance begins to fade. This marks the initial step toward genuine knowledge. As Anekanta illuminates our understanding, it begins to dissolve incorrect knowledge by clearing the layers of misconceptions and deeply ingrained prejudices.

Through Anekanta, ego is gradually diminished. When we internalize the profound teaching that truth is God, we no longer see ourselves as the centre of all things. In the presence of absolute truth, we feel humbled – like a tiny particle in the vastness of existence. This humility becomes the foundation of true surrender. Ego cannot survive where there is the realization of truth's vastness and divinity.

With this surrender, we no longer stand as obstacles to the truth. Instead, we offer ourselves at its feet, fully devoted and receptive. We stop defending our biases and begin living in alignment with the truth.

Yet, a fundamental issue within our own Jain community is this: we are often willing to bow at the feet of the Tirthankar, but not at the feet of truth. This contradiction exists despite the Tirthankar's own declaration that truth itself is God.

Until we learn to see truth as divine and worthy of reverence — just as we do with the image of the Tirthankar — we will continue to struggle with the same inner barriers. Anekanta offers us not just a philosophical lens, but a spiritual practice — a way to live with openness, humility, and surrender in the pursuit of truth.

What if truth exists in other religions as well?

Answer: Wherever truth exists — even if only in part — we must accept that, to that extent, the essence of the Divine is present there. The belief that only my religion holds the exclusive truth is, in reality, a form of attachment. When the principle of Anekanta enters our life, this attachment begins to dissolve naturally.

Attachment means being mentally or emotionally stuck in one perspective. Anekanta, by its very nature, does not allow us to remain stuck anywhere. It teaches us to move beyond boundaries, to see value even in differing viewpoints, and to understand that truth is not limited to one form, faith, or philosophy.

As we embrace Anekanta, our selfishness begins to fade. This happens because Anekanta broadens our perspective and makes our hearts more open and generous. Without such openness and expansiveness of heart, one cannot truly step into the realm of Anekanta. The deeper your understanding grows, the more your selfish tendencies naturally dissolve.

Moreover, balanced wisdom is essential to grasp the true essence of Anekanta. Without it, one may either blindly follow or rigidly reject. But once Anekanta is internalized, there is no longer a need to follow anyone blindly. With a well-balanced intellect, the under-standing you arrive at through self-inquiry becomes your truth.

Anekanta also reduces the power of temptations. The joy of discovering and experiencing truth is so profound and fulfilling that material pleasures begin to seem shallow in comparison. You become inwardly content, and worldly temptations gradually lose their grip.

Finally, Anekanta leads to the resolution of intolerance. It nurtures a calm and accepting mind, capable of listening to and reflecting on diverse opinions without agitation. Even if our current understanding is incomplete, Anekanta gives us the ability to connect fragments of truth from different sources and build a more complete picture.

In essence, Anekanta is not just about intellectual acceptance of multiple viewpoints. It is a transfor-mative way of being — one that dissolves attachment, selfishness, temptation, and intolerance, while opening the heart to a higher, more inclusive experience of truth.

The Parable of the Blind Men and the Elephant: A Lesson in Anekanta

The ancient saints offer a profound and illustrative example to explain the nature of limited perception and the value of Anekanta.

Six blind men once approached an elephant. Being blind, they could not see the animal — they had only their sense of touch to rely on. Whatever each person touched became their reality, their truth.

In this analogy, vision represents omniscience — the ability to perceive the entire reality directly. Since we are not omniscient, in that sense, we are all blind. We do not see truth in its totality. Instead, we rely on something external to guide us — this is where Shastra (scripture) comes in. Scripture is like the blind man's hand — our tool to feel our way toward the truth.

Those who possess direct realization or self-realized knowledge have no need for scripture. But in the absence of direct vision, we explore truth through scriptures, much like a blind person explores the elephant through touch.

Now imagine what happens when these six blind men attempt to describe the elephant after touching different parts:

- One touches the ear and declares, "The elephant is like a fan."
- Another feels the trunk and says, "It is like a sugarcane."
- A third grabs the tusk, "It's sharp like a blade."
- The fourth, holding the leg, insists, "It's a pillar or a barrel."
- The fifth, feeling the tail, says, "It is like a rope."
- The sixth touches the body, proclaiming, "The elephant is like a ship."

Each one is convinced that their experience is the complete truth. A debate arises — whose elephant is right and whose is wrong?

From their individual perspectives, all of them are right. But none of them have the complete truth. Then enters a wise person with sight. Observing the situation, they calmly state:

"You are all correct. What each of you has described is a part of the elephant. If you combine all your perceptions, you will begin to understand the whole elephant."

The Deeper Message

Just like these blind men, none of us possess omniscience. What we have are scriptures and limited perception, which help us grasp only parts of the vast truth. Some may perceive the elephant as a fan, others as a rope — each forming their own belief, sect, tradition, or philosophical system based on that limited experience.

And herein lies the root of religious division and ideological conflict. Each group clings to their version of the truth and resists any notion that it might be incomplete. But how can we claim our experience is the only valid one, when it's based on partial understanding?

Anekanta teaches us to recognize this very limitation. It urges us to appreciate the partial truth in every viewpoint, and to remain open to integrating multiple perspectives. Only then can we move closer to the complete truth.

The Resolution Lies in Anekanta

The resolution to our fragmented understanding of truth lies in the principle of Anekanta. Only Anekanta can guide us toward a more complete and inclusive perception of reality.

Anekanta does not ask you to deny what you already know or believe. It affirms that you have understood may very well be true — but it may not be the whole truth. Anekanta invites you to broaden your vision, to recognize that just as you hold a part of the truth, others may also hold theirs. From one perspective, you may be right; and from another, someone else may also be right.

The Hut and the Light: A Metaphor for Partial Truth

To explain this, our scriptures and sages have offered numerous metaphors. One such metaphor (analogy) is the hut and the light:

Imagine we are all sitting in separate huts. These huts are enclosed — no windows, and the doors are shut. Suddenly, in your hut, the grass roof shifts slightly, allowing a ray of sunlight to enter. The hut lights up, and you feel delighted. You can now see things clearly.

Excited by this revelation, you share the joy with your neighbour, telling them about the light in your hut. But the neighbour replies, "Light has entered my hut too." Suddenly, a subtle joy turns into discomfort. A question arises — whose light is real?

What was meant to be a celebration of truth becomes a debate over authenticity. In arguing whose light is true and whose is false, we forget the source of all light — the sun. Your light is real, but it alone is not complete. Your neighbour's light is real, but not complete either. The sun of omniscience shines on all, but when its rays become a subject of ownership and comparison, we drift further from the very truth we seek.

Anekanta helps us to move beyond these debates, urging us to pursue the full and universal light—not remain attached to our limited beam.

The Necklace of Principles: Siddhasen Diwakarji's Vision

Shri Siddhasen Diwakarji, in his Jain treatise Sanmatitarka, presents another powerful analogy.

He describes a necklace of gemstones — a collection of precious stones like the cat's eye, ruby, emerald, sapphire, and more. Each stone, when examined individually, holds its own value. But when strung together in a particular sequence to form a necklace, the collective brilliance far exceeds the sum of the individual stones.

Why? Because the radiance of each gemstone is enhanced by its relative position to the others. One gem's shine reflects and amplifies the brilliance of the next. In the same way, our philosophical principles are like these gemstones. You may hold one, I may hold another. Each has merit. Each has beauty. But none are complete by themselves.

When these principles are connected using the thread of Anekanta, they form a cohesive, radiant philosophy — a necklace of understanding that glows brighter than any singular view. The value of isolated truths is limited, but together, through Anekanta, their combined wisdom shines with extraordinary depth.

In Conclusion

Anekanta does not diminish your truth; it completes it. It does not ask you to surrender your insights; it asks you to recognize the insights of others. By doing so, it opens the path to unity without uniformity, to truth without ego, and to spirituality without division.

The Philosophical Foundation of Anekanta

Jain philosophy is not something entirely new or alienated from other traditions. Rather, it is a balanced amalgamation of diverse perspectives — an inclusive approach that seeks harmony among seemingly conflicting views. This harmonizing principle is known as Anekanta, and its seeds are scattered throughout the Agams (the sacred Jain scriptures).

While the Agams contain references to Anekanta, they do not offer a systematic explanation of the concept. The great sages and Acharyas who came after did us a tremendous service by elaborating and refining its philosophical framework.

Pioneers of Anekanta Philosophy

The first major contribution to the structured formulation of Anekanta was made by *Acharya Siddhasen Diwakarji*. His works — *Sanmatitarka*, *Nyayavatara*, and

Batrisabatrisi — laid the founda-tional stones for Anekanta within the realm of Indian logic and philosophy. He presented Anekanta as a coherent and comprehensive system of thought.

Following him, *Acharya Samantabhadra* refined and expanded Anekanta further through his significant texts, such as the *Devagama Stotra*. From that point onward, a rich tradition of scholars, Acharyas, and philosophers continued to build upon and deepen the understanding of Anekanta.

Unity Across Jain Traditions

It is truly remarkable that, despite centuries of development and the existence of two major sects — Shwetambar and Digambar — the philosophical core of Anekanta remains 99% aligned across both traditions. Whether in terms of theory, presentation, values, or conclusions, Anekanta exhibits a striking consistency.

Each tradition has produced towering intellectuals who fortified this philosophy:

- In the Shwetambar tradition: *Acharya Haribhadrasuri*, *Vadidevsuri Maharaj*, *Kalikalsarvagna Hemchandracharya*, *Malayagiri Maharaj*, and *Upadhyay Shri Yashovijayji* — all renowned for their expertise in logic and justice.

- In the Digambar tradition: *Bhatt Akalankadev*, *Vidyananda Swami*, and *Manikyachandra* emerged as legendary philosophers, especially in the field of Nyaya (logic) and Tarka (reasoning).

These scholars not only enriched their own traditions but also drew inspiration from one another, strengthening Anekanta through mutual respect and scholarly dialogue.

Glorious Example of Cross-Tradition Reverence

One particularly heartening example of inter-traditional respect is the text *Ashtasahasri*, a significant treatise on Anekanta from the Digambar tradition. *Upadhyay Shri Yashovijayji*, a distinguished Shwetambar philosopher, was so moved by its depth that he composed a commentary on it.

He began his commentary with a profound statement:

"The Tirthankar has taught us that wherever a fragment of truth is found, one must bow before it."

He acknowledged the light of truth he saw in *Ashtasahasri*, and that recognition inspired him to engage deeply with the text. In a moment of philosophical clarity, he declared:

"To believe that something cannot be true simply because it comes from someone else — what greater falsehood could there be?"

This powerful sentiment embodies the spirit of Anekanta — a willingness to bow before truth, no matter where it originates.

Conclusion

Anekanta is not merely a doctrine — it is a living philosophy that encourages openness, humility, and integration. Its strength lies not just in its logic, but in its spiritual maturity — the ability to see truth beyond ego, beyond identity, and beyond ownership. Thanks to the contributions of sages from both Jain traditions, Anekanta today stands as a shining example of philosophical unity, inclusivity, and depth.

Anekanta: The Forgotten Inheritance

We are indeed fortunate to have inherited Ahinsa (non-violence) so naturally as a part of our Jain tradition. Yet, it is our misfortune that we did not inherit Anekanta with the same ease and emphasis. We received the Navkar Mantra effortlessly repeated, revered, and remembered. But no one held our hand and guided us toward the pursuit of complete truth. As a result, the Jain community advanced significantly in terms of conduct, but remained impoverished in intellectual depth.

This gap between behaviour and understanding has widened over time — and continues to grow. While we may not be able to erase this gap entirely, we can reduce it, and our sincere effort must be directed toward that purpose.

Anekanta and Kevalgyan: Touching Complete Truth

Only Anekanta and Kevalgyan (omniscience) have the capacity to touch the complete truth. No other form of knowledge — neither worldly wisdom nor religious scripture — can fully access that realm.

- Kevalgyan perceives Sakal Arth — all aspects of reality, simultaneously and without limitation.
- Anekanta helps us understand and express those aspects in a comprehensive and inclusive manner.

The term Sakal signifies completeness, and it is this completeness that Anekanta seeks to approach.

However, there's a fascinating distinction: Kevalgyan allows one to see the complete truth — but it cannot be expressed in words. To articulate the truth seen through Kevalgyan, one must rely on Syadvad. In this way:

- Kevalgyan is the method of realization,
- Syadvad is the method of expression.

Without Syadvad, others cannot understand or experience what Kevalgyan reveals.

Truth: Complete in Vision, Fragmented in Expression

Even the Tirthankar — the one who has attained Kevalgyan — must express the truth through Naya, or partial perspectives. Why?

Because truth can only be spoken sequentially, not simultaneously. Although the Tirthankar perceives all reality at once, He cannot express all of it at once. The sequence of speech cannot be bypassed, even by the omniscient. Hence, when truth is shared, it is imparted in fragments.

Now imagine: if the Tirthankar presents ten aspects of the truth, and ten people each understand only one aspect, those ten may form ten different sects, each believing they alone have understood the full message.

This is the human tendency — to cling to fragments.

The Lock and the Ten Keys: An Analogy

Consider a lock that requires ten keys to open. Each individual receives one key from their ancestors, who tell them, "This is the key to the treasure." Proudly, each person holds up their key, believing it to be the ultimate truth.

But when someone says, "Brother, there are nine others holding the remaining keys," the response is defensive: "Those must be fake keys. My father gave me the real one."

In this, we lose the essence of what the key is for — not to be worshipped, but to unlock the treasure inside.

Syadvad: From Means to Goal

This is the transformative value of Syadvad. It shifts our focus from the means to the goal.

Acharya Haribhadrasuriji Maharaj asked a profound question: "Where do we all want to go?" The answer: Moksha (liberation). On that, there is no disagreement.

But the moment the question changes to "How do we reach Moksha?" — the disputes begin. Will liberation be attained this way or that way? Will it be attained through this path or that path?"

All disputes are about the means (Sadhan) – not the goal (Sadhya). Anekanta reminds us: the means can vary; the goal remains one.

The Real Value Lies in the Treasure, Not the Key

Anekanta teaches us that the value of a key lies not in the key itself, but in the lock it opens and the treasure it reveals.

We have become entangled in glorifying the key. We fight over the key. We compare keys. We refuse to believe that other keys may exist.

But the treasure remains unopened.

Understanding this is the essence of Anekanta.

In Conclusion

- Kevalgyan sees the complete truth.
- Syadvad expresses it.
- Anekanta embraces its many perspectives.

Let us not remain stuck in partial understandings, clinging to fragments, defending what we were handed. Instead, let us seek to combine the keys, unlock the treasure, and move together toward the goal of liberation.

Anekanta and the Four Pillars of Truth

Anekanta equips us with four essential elements necessary for attaining the complete truth. Without the integration of these four, truth remains inaccessible. Let us understand each one in detail:

1. *Neutrality (Madhyasthata)*

Remain impartial and unbiased. Often, our judgments are clouded by preconceived ideas or emotional leanings. We may unknowingly favour one side or person due to attachments or prior beliefs. True neutrality demands complete fairness, a mind free from favouritism, and the absence of a "soft corner" for anyone. Without neutrality, evaluation becomes distorted, and truth is compromised.

2. *Curiosity (Jignasa)*

Develop a genuine desire to seek the truth. Without curiosity, there is no motivation to question or explore. The thirst for truth is the fuel that drives intellectual inquiry. Only when you want to know can you move toward discovering. Curiosity is the spark that initiates the journey.

3. *Critical Analysis (Samalochana)*

Engage in discernment and logical evaluation. This involves analysing every viewpoint, identifying what is true and what is not. It means placing ideas on the scale of reason and experience, using intellect to differentiate and refine. Without analysis, opinions remain unchecked and understanding shallow.

4. *Wisdom (Pragnata)*

Possess the intellect to harmonize the other three. Wisdom is the foundation that supports neutrality, fuels curiosity, and sharpens analysis. Without wisdom, neutrality becomes passive, curiosity becomes aimless, and analysis becomes superficial. All three depend on wisdom to function effectively.

The Role of Anekanta

Anekanta nurtures and develops all four qualities within us:

- If they are absent, it instils them.
- If they are present, it strengthens and refines them.

When the intellect is shaped by Anekanta, the mind naturally becomes analytical, reflective, and inquisitive. Upon receiving any information, you instinctively begin to ask:

"What is the perspective behind this? What might be the broader context?"

Anekanta also sharpens wisdom, making your understanding as precise and effortless as a knife slicing through butter. With clarity comes enjoyment —as each fragment of truth is grasped, the desire to explore further becomes a source of joy.

And most importantly, neutrality becomes second nature. Anekanta makes it impossible to stay rigid or biased — it teaches you to listen, reflect, and rise above attachment.

In Conclusion

Truth is not attained by intellect alone, nor by devotion alone. It requires a harmony of: 1. Neutrality 2. Curiosity 3. Critical Analysis 4. Wisdom

Anekanta is the philosophy that cultivates all four, leading us even closer to the completeness of truth.

Understanding Variation Through Anekanta

Question: If the words of the Tirthankar are the same for everyone, and every Jain accepts them as true, why is there so much variation in Jain teachings?

Answer: The variation does not stem from the truth of the words, but from the interpretation of those truths. Unlike certain other traditions — such as the Brahminical tradition — where some scriptures may be openly rejected, this has never occurred in Jainism. No Jain has ever said, "I do not accept these words." This is because rejecting even a single teaching is considered Mithyatva (falsehood).

Every Jain accepts the words of the Tirthankar as truth. The differences arise from how these words are interpreted through individual intellect and perception. Each person understands only a fragment of the complete truth. These fragmented understandings lead to divergent interpretations, and over time, these interpretations have created variations within the tradition.

Anekanta bridges this gap — it takes us beyond individual interpretations and toward the deeper, unified essence of the truth.

On the Statement: 'God is Truth'

Question: Is the statement 'God is truth' true or false?

Answer: The statement is not false. From a relative perspective, it holds truth. However, for precision, it should be expressed as:

“God, who reveals the truth, is truth.”

Truth, in its absolute form (Nirapeksha Satya), cannot be confined within such simplified expressions. The original phrase, while meaningful, lacks philosophical clarity when used in an absolute sense.

Truth Has No Fear of Examination

Truth does not fear inquiry. In fact, it welcomes being tested. If something fears examination, then it is not truth.

Anything presented as truth should be weighed on the scales of logic and reason. Truth provides a sense of fearlessness. If it cannot withstand critical analysis, it cannot be called truth.

The Role of Attachment and Selfishness

Our unwillingness to change opinions often stems from two sources:

- Attachment (Mamatva) to our opinions – where we have invested our identity and pride in a particular view.
- Blind selfishness – which is often directed toward a person or object, making us resistant to any truth that might challenge that connection.

Both attachments lead to a rigid mindset, preventing openness to truth.

Anekanta Must Be Taught Early

Our efforts to teach truth usually begin too late, when a child has already formed fixed ideas. Just as we naturally teach a child not to harm even an ant, instilling the values of Ahinsa, we must also begin early in imparting Anekanta — the art of open, balanced thinking.

Today, many mothers successfully engage children in rituals and non-violence, but lack the tools to teach how to understand truth. As a result, children grow up with a shallow perspective, unable to hold space for diverse viewpoints.

Reforming Our Pathshalas

Our Pathshalas (religious schools) must evolve. Currently, many focus on memorizing texts, rituals, and shlokas, but do not adequately convey the philosophical foundations of Jainism.

If we want children to develop faith in karma, or to grasp the subtle essence of the soul, then we must teach Anekanta. Without Anekanta:

- Karma remains misunderstood,
- The soul remains abstract,
- And truth becomes rigid and sectarian.

Therefore, it is essential that Anekanta and philosophical thinking be integrated into religious education.

The Gift of Anekanta: A New Way of Listening

Even a basic understanding of Anekanta transforms how we approach spiritual teachings. You begin to listen to any discourse – regardless of tradition or speaker – and extract what is meaningful for your own growth. You stop asking,

"Why is this being said from only one viewpoint?" Instead, you learn to take what is useful and leave the rest.

Even when encountering scriptures that may be filled with misconceptions, a soul enriched with Anekanta can find nourishment for spiritual progress.

Be Like the Honeybee

The Tirthankar teaches: Be like a honeybee.

The honeybee does not discriminate. Whether it lands on a lotus, rose, or jasmine, each with its own fragrance and form, it knows to extract only the nectar.

Similarly, the seeker guided by Anekanta does not become entangled in differences. Instead, they ask:

"What here is useful for the growth of my soul?"

This ability to extract essence — to see value in all traditions, teachings, and perspectives — is the true gift of Anekantvad.

Anekantvad: Navigating Truth with Balance and Perspective

Question: What if the other person is unwilling to accept the truth? Should we give up?

Answer: The Tirthankar teaches that truth must not be shared indiscriminately. Even in presenting the truth, one must follow the principles of Anekanta.

Truth should only be shared with those who are prepared, receptive, and capable of understanding it. If someone lacks the capacity to grasp it, truth should not be forced upon them. Clear boundaries must be maintained.

Let everyone practice their faith in their own way — just ensure that their practice does not harm eternal values.

We all exist within the realm of potential truth, which is an evolving process. As we begin to understand and apply even small fragments of that truth in our conduct, the path ahead gradually becomes clearer. Truth reveals itself progressively.

Question: If the greatness of the Tirthankar's words is that everyone understands them in their own language, then why doesn't everyone follow the same religion?

Answer: The act of listening happens in three stages:

- **Hearing** – the physical reception of sound.
- **Understanding** – mentally grasping the meaning.
- **Acceptance** – internalizing and living by it.

Everyone may hear the Tirthankar's words, but understanding depends on one's intellect, and acceptance depends on one's inner capacity and spiritual maturity.

Just as hearing a foreign language doesn't guarantee comprehension, so too spiritual truth must be both understood and accepted, and the latter two vary greatly from person to person.

We do not walk on the complete truth, but we move toward it. Our conscience reassures us that we are on the right path.

Question: What if, in striving for truth, we unknowingly hold on to false beliefs?

Answer: Merely having an incorrect understanding doesn't make one an Ekantvadi (one-sided thinker). If the intention is pure and truth-seeking, then the pursuit still aligns with Anekantvad.

On the path toward Samyak Darshan (right vision), it is natural to hold some false beliefs, especially in the absence of omniscience. However, as long as the effort is guided by right intention and perspective, understanding becomes clearer over time, and falsehood is gradually shed.

A seeker of truth may misunderstand, but not in a rigid or one-sided way.

Only when someone holds a belief without openness to inquiry, assuming it to be the sole truth without testing it, does it fall into Ekantvad. Anekantvad safeguards us when we approach truth through multiple perspectives.

Truth, Sin, and Virtue – All Are Contextual

There is no action that is inherently and absolutely a sin or a virtue. Everything depends on context — when, why, and how the act was performed.

Take the example of Vastupal, a great Jain soul who is said to have killed thousands, yet attained Mahavideha and is progressing toward Moksha in the same lifetime. How is this possible?

Because he acted with a higher spiritual purpose — not from personal emotion or selfishness.

Contrast this with someone who slaps another in anger. Though it appears trivial, the karmic bondage from that slap could be heavier than that of Vastupal's actions, because it was done without Anekanta and driven by ego or aggression.

Anekantvad in Conduct: Utsarg and Apavad

In Jainism, Anekantvad doesn't just apply to philosophy — it applies to conduct as well, through the principles of: Utsarg – the general rule and Apavad – the exception.

The very presence of exceptions proves that no conduct can be judged in isolation. This is the essence of Anekantvad in behaviour. However, the ability to discern when and how to apply Anekanta in action is rare. This skill is not natural — it is a gift possessed only by the Geetarth Bhagwant, the one who has realized the deeper essence of scripture and action.

In Conclusion

- Do not force truth; offer it where there is readiness. Truth is a journey, not a destination instantly attained.
- Acceptance varies based on individual evolution.
- Misunderstanding is part of the journey — but must be free of rigidity.

- Sin and virtue are not fixed — they are contextual.
- Anekantvad is not only a thinking framework — it is also a way of living, applied in speech, action, and judgment.

Anekantvad is the compass that helps us move through the complexities of life without losing sight of the goal: truth.

Discourse 02

Reflection questions

1. Which of the nine barriers to truth do I most often struggle with — ignorance, ego, attachment, or something else?
2. How can I better develop the five faculties (intellect, information, understanding, experience, inner strength) in my pursuit of truth?
3. What effort am I making in my daily life to move beyond half-truths toward greater clarity and completeness?

Discourse 02

Short practices

Philosophical:

Throughout the day, notice moments when you speak in absolutes (e.g., "This is always like this," or "They are wrong"). Pause and ask: Could there be another layer to this truth? Make a note of at least one instance where your assumption was only partially true.

Journal:

What personal belief do you hold most strongly? Explore where it came from and how it might appear from another view.

Behavioural:

Read two contrasting articles on the same topic. Note down three truths from each.

Meditation:

Visualize climbing a mountain and seeing the same landscape from multiplc anglcs.

Image description

This image powerfully illustrates the essence of Anekanta through a radiant, many-faceted crystal surrounded by people. Each individual sees a different facet, symbolizing how truth appears varied depending on one's perspective. The light at the centre of the crystal represents the absolute truth – unchanged and pure – while the differing reflections show relative truths shaped by angles of view. Anekanta teaches that no single viewpoint can capture the whole; it is only through acknowledging multiple perspectives that we move closer to completeness.

Discourse 03

THE TRUTH BEYOND CERTAINTY

Introduction:

In a world conditioned to see everything as either true or false, Jain philosophy introduces Sambhavit Satya — the Probable Truth. Rooted in Anekanta, this principle encourages us to move beyond rigid thinking and embrace the complexity of perspectives. It teaches that truth is often contextual and relative, not absolute. While doubt reflects indecision, Syadvad represents a well-reasoned, conditional truth. Misunderstanding this difference has led to sectarianism and rigidity, even within Jainism. This article explores how Anekanta refines our intellect, balances our conduct, and leads us closer to complete truth — not by force, but through openness and equanimity.

Key theme:

This discourse dives into the tension between certainty and doubt, and how Anekanta provides a middle path. It explains that clinging to fixed beliefs creates intellectual blindness, while Anekanta cultivates a flexible outlook that adapts and evolves. Practically, it trains us to replace judgments with inquiry.

Sambhavit Satya: Understanding the Value of Probable Truth

Anekanta introduces a significant philosophical principle known as Sambhavit Satya, or Probable Truth. To grasp its depth and relevance, we must carefully differentiate it from doubt and appreciate its unique position within the framework of Syadvad.

1. The Habit of Binary Thinking

We are accustomed to interpreting any statement as either true or false. This binary approach dominates our everyday thinking, where we assume that every claim must fall into one of these two categories.

2. The Realm of Possible Truth

However, many statements we encounter do not strictly fall under the categories of truth or falsehood. Instead, they belong to the domain of Possible Truth.

For example:

"This might be the case, or it might not."

In such statements, we leave the door open to both possibilities — it could be true, or it could be false. The existence of dual possibilities without a conclusion is what characterizes Possible Truth.

3. *Doubt (Sanshay) Is Not Syadvad*

This kind of possibility is not Syadvad. It is Sanshay — doubt. When we are unable to reach a definite conclusion, we remain in a state of indecision. For instance:

"Is this Upashray (monastery) four stories or five stories tall?" "I think it could be four, but I'm not sure–it could be five."

This is not Syadvad. It reflects uncertainty. You've left both directions open without commitment. This is an example of Possible Truth, not Probable Truth.

4. *Syadvad and Probable Truth: A Key Distinction*

Syadvad deals with a different level of understanding — Probable Truth. It is not vague or uncertain. Instead, it is a decisive statement made with awareness of perspective and condition.

For example:

"This Upashray has a basement. Including the basement, it is five stories tall. Without it, it is four."

This is Syadvad. It is a contextual conclusion, not doubt. It recognizes that truth depends on how the question is framed — what is included or excluded.

5. *Difference in Opinion vs. Difference in Perspective*

Suppose two people argue — one says the Upashray is four stories tall, the other says five. If you merely say, “It could be either,” you remain undecided —that is Possible Truth, not Syadvad.

However, if you say: “Both are correct depending on the perspective: one includes the basement, the other does not,” this is Syadvad, because it is firm, contextual, and reasoned.

6. *The Misunderstanding of Syadvad*

One of the most common errors is confusing Syadvad with doubt. But Syadvad is not uncertainty. It is a deliberate and balanced conclusion drawn through proper reasoning.

Merely saying:

“It could be this or that,”

— is not Syadvad. It is indecisiveness.

7. *Doubt as a Form of Ignorance*

According to the Tirthankar, doubt (Sanshay) is a form of ignorance (Agyan). He defines three types of ignorance:

1. **Viparit Gyan** – Misconception or false knowledge
2. **Sanshay** – Indecision or doubt
3. **Anadhyavasay** – Neglect or lack of attentiveness

For example, performing Chaityavandan but being unable to recall if the deity wore a crown is Anadhyavasay — seeing without truly seeing.

All three forms — misconception, doubt, and inattentiveness — are forms of ignorance. Therefore, doubt cannot be equated with Syadvad, which is a tool for expanding knowledge, not obscuring it.

8. The Essence of Probable Truth (Sambhavit Satya)

- In Possible Truth, both directions remain open, and no decision is made.
- In Probable Truth, a reasoned decision is reached, with the awareness that it is contextual and relative.

This awareness and relativity are the core of Syadvad — and by extension, the essence of Anekanta.

The Reason for the Emergence of Sects

A question was raised: How can a philosophy that so deeply values the pursuit of complete truth give rise to so many sects? And how can there be friction among these sects? To answer this, we must first understand the origin of sect formation, and only then can we explore how Anekanta offers practical solutions to such divisions.

Acharya Shri Nemichandrasuriji Maharaj has identified seven key reasons for the emergence of sects. Historical records reveal that almost every sect formed can be traced back to one of these causes:

1. *Jealousy*

When someone's success or spiritual progress becomes intolerable to others, it creates resentment. This emotional reaction often leads to the creation of a new ideology, which gradually develops into a separate sect.

2. *Hunger for Fame*

The desire for recognition, prestige, and influence can motivate individuals to carve out an independent identity. Over time, this craving can lead to the establishment of a new sect.

3. *Ideological Differences*

These arise when interpretations of scripture or traditions diverge. However, Anekanta has the power to resolve such differences, provided it is applied sincerely.

Example: Originally, Samvatsari Mahaparva was observed on Bhadarva Sud 5 (Panchami). Due to situational necessities, the observance was shifted to Sud 4 (Choth), which led to other adjustments:

- Pakkhi Pratikraman was moved from Poonam (full moon) to Chaudash (14th day).
- Chaumasi Pratikraman, traditionally on Poonam, also shifted to Chaudash.

Later, when the reason for shifting from Panchami to Choth no longer applied, some communities suggested returning to Panchami. Accordingly, one group did so and also reverted to observing Pakkhi on Poonam. However, another group resisted this change, fearing that it would disrupt the sacred calendar and lead to binding karmic consequences.

This led to ideological division, even though both interpretations had merit based on their own reasoning. Since only a Kevalgyani (omniscient being) can determine the complete truth, such differences often remain unresolved.

Anekanta offers a simple resolution: Let both practices coexist peacefully. In the same Upashray, both groups can observe their chosen form of worship without conflict. But this ideal is rarely practiced. Instead, one group insists on supremacy, leading to division — such as one sect observing Chaudash and the other Poonam.

4. *Differences in Conduct*

Minor variations in practices often exist, but rigid attachment to a particular form of conduct eventually results in the formation of sects.

5. *Perceived Insult or Disrespect*

When individuals feel that their identity, status, or contribution is being undervalued or disrespected, it can prompt them to separate and establish a new sect to protect their self-worth.

6. *Pursuit of a Specific Truth*

When someone seeks to attain a unique or specialized truth, they may formulate new methods or rituals tailored to that pursuit. Over time, these methods may evolve into a distinct sect.

7. *Contextual Necessity (Dravya–Kshetra–Kaal–Bhaav)*

Change becomes necessary based on matter (dravya), location (kshetra), time (kaal), and intent (bhaav). Even if such change is completely valid, it may not be understood or accepted by others. This leads to divergence and the creation of a new sect.

Understanding These Causes Through Anekanta

- The first five reasons – jealousy, fame, conduct differences, insult, and ego – are rooted in emotional and personal inclinations. These can and should be resolved through Anekanta.
- The last two reasons – contextual need and pursuit of deeper truth – are not inherently negative. They are often necessary for the progress and evolution of the religious framework.

However, individuals rarely admit to emotional causes like jealousy or insult. Instead, they mask them as ideological or conduct-related disputes. This is why Anekanta becomes essential – to recognize, respect, and integrate differing viewpoints without division.

Addressing the Roots of Sect Formation Through Anekanta

The learned masters have clarified that the last two causes for the emergence of sects – (6) the pursuit of a specific truth and (7) the need for change based on matter, place, time, or circumstances (Dravya–Kshetra–Kaal–Bhaav) are not only valid but often beneficial to the system.

These causes either guide the tradition toward higher truth or bring about necessary structural reforms to ensure its stability.

Thus, the sixth reason supports spiritual progress, while the seventh sustains organizational stability.

Both are essential for the governance and evolution of the religious framework.

In contrast, the first five causes — jealousy, hunger for fame, ideological rigidity, differences in conduct, and perceived insult — arise from personal emotions and ego-driven motives.

These can cause unnecessary division and disharmony within the tradition.

To prevent and resolve these emotional causes, the application of Anekanta is vital. When practiced sincerely and with clarity, Anekanta has the power to diffuse conflict, prevent fragmentation, and encourage peaceful coexistence.

From a psychological perspective, it's important to note that individuals rarely admit to causes such as jealousy, the desire for fame, or personal offense. Instead, when a separation occurs due to such reasons, it is often reframed as an ideological or conduct-based dispute.

The narrative typically stops at the third or fourth cause, masking the deeper emotional triggers.

However, even ideological and conduct-related differences can be harmonized through Anekanta. Anekanta teaches that people with divergent beliefs or practices can still coexist peacefully.

It is neither necessary to form separate groups nor to criticize or invalidate the views of others.

The Proper Method of Applying Logic

One of the greatest challenges in the realm of intellect is learning to apply logic (Tark) correctly. Anything that falls within the domain of thought and reasoning must be understood through proper logical analysis. The essential principle is this:

Apply logic with sincerity and impartiality, and accept whatever truth emerges from that process as the truth.

However, the common mistake humans make is to first form a rigid conclusion — a preconceived notion of what they believe is true — and then use logic not to discover the truth, but to justify that belief.

The Horse and Cart Analogy

The learned masters offer a clear metaphor: "Always place the horse before the cart."

In this analogy:

- The horse represents logic
- The cart represents assumptions

We are advised to let logic lead, and allow our assumptions to follow wherever logic takes us. However, what often happens is the reverse — we place the cart before the horse. We start with a fixed assumption and then force our logic to prove it right. This backward approach does not serve truth — it only defends ego.

The Tirthankar refers to this misuse as Kutark — fallacious logic.

Samyak Tark vs. Kutark

- Samyak Tark (Right Reasoning): Logic that is used to discover truth, free from bias.
- Kutark (Fallacious Logic): Logic used to defend a preconceived conclusion, regardless of its validity.

If you accept a belief first and then attempt to justify it through reasoning, it is not truth-seeking. It is ego-protection disguised as intellect.

The Web of Fallacy

Today, many systems and individuals are entangled in Kutark. Those with rigid mindsets attach their intellect to pre-decided positions and then employ reasoning not to explore, but to defend. In contrast, those who apply unbiased logic first, and accept whatever emerges as truth, walk the path of genuine discovery.

The Role of Anekanta

This is where Anekanta becomes transformative. It liberates us from the compulsion to defend inherited or preferred ideas. It teaches us to:

- Begin with open inquiry
- Let logic guide us
- Accept truth in its contextual, many-sided form.

When we practice Anekanta, we not only approach truth with humility and balance, but also cultivate equanimity (Samata) — the capacity to remain centered, undisturbed by differing views.

Anekanta does not ask us to abandon logic. It asks us to apply it rightly — without bias, without ego, and without preconditions.

The Three Dimensions of Equanimity (Samata)

The practical application of Anekanta is equanimity, or Samata. It empowers you to cultivate such deep inner balance that no belief, idea, or opinion can disturb or dominate you.

1. ***Equanimity Toward Beings***

This is the most commonly understood form: to not hold attachment (Raag) or aversion (Dvesh) toward any living being. When this equanimity reaches its highest expression, Ahinsa (non-violence) arises naturally—born from the realization that the same soul exists in all.

2. ***Equanimity Toward Personal Experiences***

This form of Samata means to remain undisturbed by what happens to us — to avoid reacting with Raag or Dvesh to favourable or unfavourable circumstances. At its peak, this leads to Madhyasthata (neutrality) — a state of calm detachment.

3. ***Equanimity Toward Beliefs and Viewpoints***

The most challenging dimension of Samata is to be free of Raag-Dvesh toward opinions and doctrines. This is the very essence of Anekanta. It requires letting go of rigid intellectual attachment and embracing multiple perspectives with openness.

The Root of Fanaticism and the Cure of Anekanta

Most people diligently practice the first two forms of Samata, yet neglect the third. Why? Because we often cling to our version of truth, convinced of its superiority. This rigid attachment, though disguised as devotion, leads to fanaticism.

For example, one might say: “I follow only the scriptures. I will stand alone if I must, but I will not deviate.”

While this may sound principled, it reflects rigidity, not clarity. Syadvad breaks this fanaticism, and Anekanta dissolves rigidity. A true practitioner of Anekanta is firm but never fanatic, steadfast but never narrow-minded.

Sharing Truth Without Imposition

A fanatic does not stop at personal practice. They attempt to convince or convert others and, if not accepted, label dissenters as wrong. In contrast, an Anekantavadi may share their understanding, but never impose it. If someone differs, they acknowledge:

“That is your truth from your perspective. I will live by what I have understood.”

Such mutual respect is rare, but essential.

The Trap of Attachment to Method

The goal is liberation, not loyalty to a technique. But people become attached to methods, mistaking them for the goal itself. This has repeated in every lifetime. We cling to names, beliefs, rituals, and lose sight of the soul's freedom.

Anekanta teaches: Do not become attached — not even to your own thoughts, practices, or doctrines.

The Missing Practice of Anekanta

Ask yourself honestly: Do I practice Anekanta with the same dedication I show toward Ahinsa and Madhyasthya?

We reflect deeply on non-violence. We deliberate on neutrality. But when it comes to Anekanta, we rarely engage. Our spiritual efforts will accelerate when we truly strive toward the peak of Anekanta.

In Summary: The Path Forward

- Ahinsa arises from equanimity toward beings.
- Madhyasthya arises from equanimity toward circumstances.
- Anekanta arises from equanimity toward beliefs.

All three are interdependent pillars of spiritual growth. If practiced sincerely, they lead to true inner freedom and the purification of the soul.

The Danger of One-Sidedness: Words of Shri Siddhasen Diwakarji

Shri Siddhasen Diwakarji offers a profound warning to those who equate devotion to the system (Shasan) with mastery of its principles:

"Merely being devoted to the system does not make you a knower of its philosophy. Just because you say, 'I am loyal to the system, so what I say must be accepted,' does not make it so. Devotion and knowledge are two different things."

Even acquiring some scriptural understanding does not automatically qualify one to deliver discourses or guide others. Until one deeply understands Anekanta, they cannot wield the intellectual balance and impartiality needed to speak without bias. Without this foundation, every discourse becomes one-sided—and the system suffers the most from such narrow representations.

If a person leans entirely toward Vyavhar Nay (the practical standpoint) or Nishchay Nay (the absolute standpoint), they distort the balance of Jain philosophy and harm the system in both cases.

Even discussions around Arya culture divide people: Some believe everything in the past was ideal. Others argue for abandoning the past to adopt modernity.

But when a teacher becomes anchored to a single ideology, their discourse inevitably becomes divisive, creating discord among followers and fragmenting the unity of the community.

The Need for Anekanta as a Foundation

The biggest challenge facing the Sangh (community) today is that it has become a gathering of followers rather than a collective of seekers.

A follower is someone devoted to an individual or ideology, often saying: "I am their devotee," or "This is my Guru."

This attachment leads to pride, and pride breeds contempt toward others who do not share the same path. As a result, the vital quality of equanimity (Samata) is lost.

Why Anekanta Is Essential for Ahinsa

The Tirthankar has declared: "Without Anekanta, true Ahinsa cannot be practiced."

This may seem surprising at first — how are thought (Anekanta) and conduct (Ahinsa) related?

The answer lies in human psychology: Without Anekanta, one begins to harbour judgment and contempt toward others' beliefs or practices. This judgment gives rise to Raag (attachment) and Dvesh (aversion) — and where these emotions exist, Ahinsa is no longer possible.

Thus, Anekanta is not optional — it is indispensable for practicing true non-violence.

Knowledge Without Anekanta: A Dangerous Combination

Some individuals become repositories of scriptural knowledge — like living hard drives, full of texts, terminology, and teachings. They are respected, followed, and revered. But if they have not imbibed Anekanta, their scholarship becomes dangerous.

Despite being Bahushrut (well-read), if they fail to grasp the spirit of plurality and openness, they become enemies of the very Shasan they claim to serve.

Why? Because they preach Ekanta (one-sidedness) under the banner of Jainism, and mislead followers into dogma, not truth. Both the speaker and the audience fall into the trap of fanaticism cloaked in devotion.

Anekanta Must Be the Starting Point

To prevent this decline, Anekanta must be established as the foundation of spiritual education — not something we learn later in life.

One must begin the journey with Anekanta — with openness, intellectual humility, and breadth of perspective.

Without it, even the purest devotion or deepest study lacks balance and leads to fragmentation.

The Benefits of Syadvad

Various scriptures and learned masters have described numerous benefits of Syadvad, the principle of conditioned or relative truth. Some of the most profound insights include:

1. *Realization of One's Capability (Patrata)*

One learned master notes that Syadvad enables an individual to assess their own capacity to comprehend truth. By analysing situations and statements through the lens of Syadvad, a person becomes more aware of their intellectual limitations and potential. This self-awareness marks the beginning of genuine growth.

2. *Understanding the Limits of Our Tools of Knowledge*

Syadvad reveals the inherent limitations of the seven tools we rely upon to acquire knowledge: The five senses (sight, sound, smell, taste, touch) and the mind, which draws from: Personal experiences and Scriptural learning.

All seven tools are incomplete and limited. For instance, science confirms that humans cannot hear the full spectrum of sound, or perceive all light wavelengths.

Our mental experiences are fragmented: some inherited, some karmic (from past lives), and some learned.

Scriptures too, while revered, are not direct realizations but guides — like a blind man's stick.

Syadvad helps us recognize the partial nature of our knowledge and inspires us to strive toward Kevalgyan (omniscience) — the infinite, complete tool of perception.

Anekanta and the Nature of True Detachment (Vairagya)

Without Anekanta, detachment is often mis-guided. It typically takes one of two flawed forms:

1. *Pain-Driven Detachment*

This arises from suffering – when people feel defeated or exhausted by the world, they seek refuge in religion or ascetic life. However, this detachment is rooted in escape, not understanding.

2. *Attachment-Driven Detachment*

Even more dangerous, this arises from rigid ideological attachment. A person may take Diksha (initiation) or engage in severe religious practices driven not by truth but by fanaticism.

This "Jehadi mindset" (mindset of extreme ideological attachment) is not limited to any one religion. While some may express it through violence, others express it through harsh words, dogma, and condemnation. Whether one strikes with a stone or with speech, the intent to harm makes both actions equivalent.

The Essence of Knowledge-Based Detachment

True detachment, as envisioned in Jain philosophy, emerges from knowledge and Anekanta: It is not pain-driven. It is not ideology-driven. It is a sincere pursuit of absolute truth, grounded in the realization of the soul's potential.

When this pursuit turns inward, it leads to Keval Darshan (self-realization). When expanded outward, it manifests as Kevalgyan, embracing the entire universe across the 14 Rajloks.

Such detachment, born of clarity and aspiration, is only possible through the lens of Anekanta. Without it, detachment will inevitably fall into one of the two misguided forms.

The Role of Syadvad in Spiritual Practice (Aradhana)

Question: Should Aradhana (spiritual practice) be rooted in faith or in the pursuit of truth?

Answer: If one is a Baljeev (novice), the journey naturally begins with faith. But this faith must evolve. As the seeker progresses, faith should transform into inquiry, and inquiry into insight. The teachings may begin in Shraddha (faith), but they must culminate in Satya (truth).

How Syadvad Refines Our Understanding of Truth

Our senses perceive only forms — not meaning. E.g., If the word Anekanta is written in Chinese, we may see the characters but not comprehend them.

Sound is heard by the ears, but the mind assigns meaning, based on:

- Past experiences
- Scriptural impressions
- Sanskaras (imprints from previous lives)

Two people reading the same sentence can interpret it differently, depending on their inner impressions and mental clarity.

Syadvad helps us recognize this variation. It reminds us that:

- Perception is filtered through limitation.
- Interpretation is shaped by past conditioning.
- Realization of truth is gradual and evolving.
- Conclusion: Syadvad as a Gateway to Kevalgyan

Syadvad not only helps us respect multiple perspectives, but also deepens our desire to transcend partiality. It reveals:

- The limits of our tools
- The imperfection of assumptions
- The necessity of humility
- And the path toward complete knowledge

When practiced with sincerity, Syadvad and Anekanta guide us not only to truth, but to freedom from the ego that clings to it.

The Proportion of Truth in Knowledge: Anekanta's Analytical Lens

What is false remains false, yet the Tirthankar explains that 66% of any knowledge we acquire is inherently true. This might seem perplexing at first, but let's break it down to understand how this principle works.

Breaking Down Knowledge into Three Parts: In any act of knowing, there are three essential components:

1. ***Pramāta*** – The knower (the one who knows)
2. ***Prameya*** – The object of knowledge (what is known)
3. ***Pramiti*** – The act of knowing (the process of knowing)

Let's take a simple example:

You say, "I know this is a pot."

- The phrase "I know" expresses an awareness of knowing, which is always true — regardless of what is being known.

- Thus, the Pramāta (I) and Pramiti (knowing) are each 33% of the statement, and both are inherently true.
- The third part — Prameya (the pot) — can be true or false, depending on whether it is, in fact, a pot.

Hence, in any knowledge claim:

- 66% is inherently true (the act of knowing and the knower)
- 33% may be true or false, based on the accuracy of the object perceived.

An Example: Seeing Two Moons

Suppose a person with an eye disorder sees two moons and says, "I know there are two moons in the sky."

Even though the object of knowledge is flawed, the statements:

- "I" (Pramāta) – the self-awareness
- "know" (Pramiti) – the act of perception remain valid.

In the remaining 33%:

- The sky is indeed the backdrop (true)
- The object resembles a moon (true)

- The error lies in seeing two instead of one.

Thus, even the false part contains partial truth, and the total statement still holds a significant proportion of validity.

Falsehood is Rarely Absolute

The Tirthankar teaches us to analyse the proportion of truth and falsehood in any statement.

We live in a world where:

- No statement is 100% true or 100% false.
- Decisions must be made by examining context and percentage.

For instance:

Saying "I see a pot" is technically imprecise because we usually only see the front of the pot.

The back remains unseen, yet we refer to the entire pot.

To be fully accurate, we would have to say:

"I see the front part of the pot."

But in daily life, we operate on practical understanding, not microscopic precision. Hence, truth and falsehood exist in degrees, not absolutes.

How Anekanta Reshapes Our Perception

Anekanta encourages us to think proportionally, not absolutely. When you start viewing the world through this lens:

- Your mindset becomes more measured.
- Your judgments become more fair.
- Your understanding becomes more nuanced.

Take this statement: "I know this person."

If asked, "Does this person have a mole on his right shoulder?", you may not know — because your knowledge is based only on what you've seen.

So, your claim is not false, but incomplete. It is a surface-level, practical understanding, not a complete one.

Conclusion

Do not rush to label statements as absolutely true or false. Instead, assess how much of them are accurate.

This approach — championed by Anekanta —invites us to embrace clarity, humility, and fairness in all areas of life.

Here is a visual representation of the Three Components of Knowledge according to Jain philosophy and Syadvad:

- Pramāta (Knower) and Pramiti (Act of Knowing) together form 66% of inherent truth.
- Prameya (Object Known) can be true or false, contributing to the remaining 34%.

This model helps us understand why every knowledge claim contains degrees of truth, not absolute certainty.

The Decline of Truth-Seeking Debates

Question: In the past, many debates ended with one side accepting the truth. Why does this rarely happen today?

Answer: *Shri Haribhadrasuri Maharaj*, along with many other ancient and modern scholars, deeply reflected on the nature and evolution of debate. They categorized debates into three types, based on the intention behind the dialogue:

1. *Truth-Oriented Debate (Driven by Curiosity)*

This is the highest form of debate — born from a genuine desire to know the truth. In such discussions:

- Both sides come prepared with their own understanding.

- They share a mutual commitment to accept the conclusion that emerges through dialogue.
- These debates often occur between guru and disciple, where the relationship allows space for surrender to wisdom.

Example:

The conversation between Gautamswami and Mahavirswami is an ideal illustration. Though Gautamswami initially entered the dialogue with the intention to win, he instantly surrendered upon realizing the depth of Mahavira's wisdom. This transformed the debate from adversarial to dialogical, and ultimately, to transformative.

2. *Power-Oriented Debate (Driven by Vijigisha – the urge to win)*

This form of debate stems from the desire to dominate the other person intellectually.

- The objective is not to arrive at truth, but to prove oneself superior.
- Though some level of integrity might still be maintained, the spirit of openness is lost.

3. Ego-Oriented Debate (Driven by dishonesty or manipulation)

This is the lowest form of debate, where:

- Winning is the only goal.
- Participants use dishonest tactics—twisting arguments, misrepresenting facts, or fabricating logic.
- The debate loses all ethical grounding and becomes a tool for intellectual violence.

Such debates are highly condemned, as they serve no spiritual or philosophical purpose.

Advice to Monks and Seekers

Jain tradition advises Sadhus (monks) to avoid such destructive debates altogether.

Whether you win or lose, the damage is inevitable — the opposing side may harbour lifelong resentment, and the spirit of equanimity (Samabhava) is lost.

Why Debates Today Don't Lead to Truth

Ask yourself honestly: Are most discussions today driven by a sincere quest for truth, or are they fuelled by ego, competitiveness, and the urge to outshine others?

Sadly, most modern debates are not about discovering or surrendering to truth — they are about defeating the other. And in such a climate, truth can never emerge.

Conclusion

Let us return to the first kind of debate — one rooted in curiosity, humility, and a shared commitment to truth. Only such dialogues are worthy of pursuit. All others, no matter how well-argued, only add to confusion and division.

The Courage to Seek Truth Through Anekanta

You must keep your mind open and be willing to seek the truth in whatever is said. This is the heart of Anekanta. From now on, whenever a scholar speaks, your role is to extract the essence of truth from their words. Apply only what resonates with you deeply and meaningfully — without feeling any compulsion to follow a particular directive. I do not ask you to walk any one path blindly. My advice is simply this: remain open, think critically, and contemplate before choosing your direction.

Unfortunately, we often hear someone say, "Do this," and we instantly act on it. This must change. Instead, pause — first know, then understand, reflect, and finally decide your own truth. Do not allow yourself to become a victim of others' beliefs. Avoid being blindly led.

The spiritual path never advocated blind submission. Never surrender your intellect. Do not cling to individuals — cling to their wisdom. One of our greatest flaws is equating understanding with devotion to the speaker. Do not assume, "This must be true because he said it." Continue your personal quest for complete truth. If you follow this, Anekanta will manifest naturally in your life. And no, I am not suggesting you become directionless or wander aimlessly.

I understand what frightens you. So far, life has felt safe and simple — you clung to someone's feet, followed their instructions, and felt secure. You believed, "Since I followed what they said, my well-being is guaranteed." But Anekanta shakes that trust, and with it comes fear. You suddenly realize the beam you were holding on to is made of sand, not stone. You begin to think:

"Now I must seek truth myself... I must reflect... I must choose for myself!" This thought is daunting, but necessary.

Why do people prefer allopathy over Ayurveda? Because allopathy gives quick solutions: a diagnosis, a prescription, and you're done. Ayurveda, on the other hand, asks you to examine your habits, understand your imbalances, and make lifestyle changes. This requires reflection and effort, which feels intimidating. You think, “Just give me the medicine!” — but Anekanta demands you to engage with the process. It asks you to be courageous in the face of effort.

Anekanta wants to eliminate that fear — the fear of exploring, the hesitation to question. Don’t ask, “What if I don’t find the truth in this lifetime?” Even if it takes seven lifetimes, the search must go on. And once found, it must be revered and practiced. Your spiritual efforts do not end with death — they continue into your next birth. Isn't it better to move forward with understanding, even slowly, than to blindly engage in ritualism without realization?

I know many fears getting lost on the way. Let me assure you — wandering is part of reaching the destination. If you stay fixed in one spot, refusing to question or move, you’ll never progress. Do not fear wandering.

Break Free from Blind Devotion

Society has long fed us a toxic belief: place the Guru above all, accept every word they say without questioning back, and surrender entirely. This mindset has done immense damage.

Such teachings were once intended for enlightened beings — the 10 Purvadhars or 14 Purvadhar Bhagwants — whose words were infallible and rooted in ultimate truth. But today, if a person still bound by ignorance asks you to surrender to him, to follow every word unquestionably, this is not acceptable.

Using scriptures to demand blind obedience and justify personal authority is a misuse of the scriptures themselves.

Balancing Faith and Intellect Through Anekanta

In conduct, follow your Guru; in thought, seek the truth.

If you lack deeper understanding, it is perfectly appropriate to follow your Guru's guidance in matters of practice. For instance, if your Guru instructs you to perform Pratikraman in a specific way, follow that sincerely. In such matters, be loyal to your lineage and customs.

But do not surrender your intellect. At the level of thought, your search for truth must remain active. Never accept beliefs blindly just because someone says, "We are right, and others are wrong." If your Guru asks you to do Pratikraman on Monday, follow that without resistance. But if they insist that those, who do it on Sunday are wrong, and you adopt that belief without examination, you fall into intellectual rigidity. Anekanta teaches us that Pratikraman on either day can be valid, depending on the perspective.

Be calm in practice and open in thought. Remain faithful in conduct, but intellectually open. This is the balance Anekanta aims to instill. Follow your Guru outwardly, but never stop questioning inwardly: What is the higher truth?

The Universal Relevance of Anekanta

Anekanta applies to all domains of life. All knowledge that we acquire is from a point of view, whereas Kevalgyan (omniscience) encompasses all points of view simultaneously. Kevalgyan sees the whole truth, but its expression is always adapted to our limited understanding. Therefore, absolute truth remains beyond our full grasp, and every truth we know comes conditioned by Anekanta.

Anekanta does not imply indecisiveness.

A common misconception is that Syadvad or Anekanta avoids making conclusions. That is not true. Once the perspective is established, what follows must be stated with clarity and conviction.

For example, saying "It can be considered the third floor if counted from the basement" is incorrect. The proper application of Anekanta is: "If counted from the basement, it is the third floor."

This statement establishes the perspective and then makes a decisive conclusion. Simply saying "It is the third floor" lacks context and thus lacks Anekanta.

The Dawn of Anekanta

No night lasts forever. In the vastness of this universe, every night is followed by dawn. Even if today, we are lost in the darkness of Monism (Ekant), the sun of Anekanta will inevitably rise — perhaps in someone's heart, in someone's Upashray, or in someone's understanding.

And yet, Anekanta must never become rigid. If Anekanta were universally adopted in a rigid form, it would transform into another Ekant, which defeats its very essence. The world exists because of duality:

- Day exists because night exists.
- Sky exists because Earth exists.
- Truth exists because falsehood exists.

Anekanta teaches us that truth and falsehood, like man and woman, are interdependent. Remove one, and the meaning of the other collapses.

The Core Question

If both Anekanta and Ekant coexist in this universe, then the real question becomes:

Will I remain trapped in rigid Monism, or will I awaken to the light of Anekanta? The goal is to manifest the sun of Anekanta within our own lives.

Sarvamat-Samabhava: Universal Acceptance of Perspectives

Jain philosophy does not promote Sarvadharma-Samabhava (universal religious acceptance), but Sarvamat-Samabhava — the universal acceptance of viewpoints or perspectives. Religion is rooted in conduct (achar), and all forms of conduct cannot be treated equally. For instance, if one were to equally accept the Muslim practice of animal sacrifice during Bakri Eid, it would become difficult for a Jain to pursue efforts like animal protection (Jivdaya). Therefore, Jainism emphasizes that all perspectives must be examined, not all practices must be accepted.

Samabhava does not mean blind equivalence. It does not imply that all beliefs hold equal truth. Rather, Sarvamat-Samabhava means that we evaluate each perspective with equal impartiality — without bias or prejudice — and accept only that part which holds truth.

The truth in each view may differ in degree, and Jain philosophy encourages us to analyse, understand, and then value each belief based on its alignment with truth.

Faith, Doubt, and the Right Starting Point

What if someone loses faith and falls into doubt?

This is common when a person begins their spiritual journey with blind faith, and that faith later collapses under scrutiny. What should be done in such cases?

The solution lies in tailoring the approach to the nature of the individual:

- If the person is logical by nature, never begin with faith. Engage them through rational discussion and begin with the principle of Anekanta.
- If the person is innocent or emotionally inclined, it is fine to start with faith — but guide them gradually toward understanding.

In today's context — where logic and questioning are valued — it is more effective to start with Anekanta and lead people to Ahinsa, rather than the other way around. Anekanta builds intellectual openness, which then makes one naturally inclined toward non-violence. Ahinsa and Anekanta are like two tusks of the same elephant — they complete each other.

Truth Over God: A Jain Perspective

- Jainism does not say "God is Truth." Instead, it says: **“सच्चं खु भगवं...”** – “Truth is God.”

- And it declares: **“स्याद्वादः सत्यलाञ्छनः”** – “Syadvad is the hallmark of Truth.”

Let these become the taglines of your mind. If you truly adopt this approach, the path of truth will naturally unfold before you.

The confusion in life arises not because truth is difficult, but because we often take the wrong direction.

Discourse 03

Reflection questions

1. Do I confuse doubt with openness? How can I practice Anekanta without falling into indecision?
2. Have I ever mistaken probable truth for absolute truth? What was the impact of that on my thinking or relationships?
3. How can I develop the intellectual humility needed to hold space for Sambhavit Satya (probable truth)?

Discourse 03

Short practices

Philosophical:

Choose a strong belief or opinion you hold. Now reframe it using "Syad" (maybe, from one perspective). Example: "This is the best solution" → "From one perspective, this could be the best solution." Notice how this change opens your thinking.

Journal:

Recall a time when you were certain but later found out you were wrong. What did it teach you about certainty?

Behavioural:

Ask a friend their view on a moral issue and practice only asking clarifying questions.

Meditation:

Focus on your breath and say – 'What I see is partial, what exists is vast.'

Image description

This image beautifully embodies Anekanta within the context of Jain philosophy and temple tradition. Monks and scholars are seen contemplating a grand temple from different angles, each viewing unique symbols and visual interpretations. The temple symbolizes absolute truth, while the surrounding panels represent diverse doctrinal insights and philosophical lenses. Anekanta teaches that truth must be explored through multiple perspectives — no single view can encompass its entirety. This scene reflects intellectual humility, reverence for varied interpretations, and the coexistence of multiple truths in pursuit of the one.

Discourse 04

ANEKANTVAD:

THE ESSENCE OF JAINISM

Introduction:

In a world shaped by inherited customs, Anekanta invites us to move beyond blind tradition toward conscious contemplation. True neutrality does not lie in passive acceptance but rather in active, unbiased inquiry — examining all perspectives with fairness before arriving at one's truth. Jain philosophy reminds us that merely following rituals without understanding is Kulachar, not true Dharma. When the intellect awakens and choice emerges, we are called to explore, reason, and refine our beliefs. Anekanta nurtures this spirit of introspection, guiding us toward respectful coexistence and deeper spiritual alignment. It teaches that steadfastness in one's truth should never turn into rigidity against others. In this lies the silent strength of neutrality — anchored in awareness, not attachment.

Key theme:

More than a concept, Anekantvad is the spiritual heartbeat of Jainism. This discourse encourages us to transcend inherited customs and engage in rational contemplation. By distinguishing between steadfast-ness and rigidity, it calls for authentic practice rooted in reflection, not just ritual.

Contemplation Beyond Tradition: The Essence of True Neutrality

Does this mean we should never question what is true and what is false? Should we blindly follow the practices we were born into, without ever examining or understanding different perspectives?

According to scriptural wisdom, until we cultivate introspection and true understanding, the religion we practice remains merely Kulachar Dharma – the inherited tradition of our lineage. True Jainism is not yet realized through such inherited practice alone. If born into a Jain family, one naturally follows Jain rituals. Had one been born into another tradition; a different path would have been followed. This is the nature of Kulachar. However, it is crucial that Kulachar does not harden into rigidity or blind fanaticism.

The moment your intellect awakens, your understanding matures, and you are presented with more than one choice, an honest and open examination becomes essential.

Once you arrive at a conclusion that resonates with your reasoning, commit to practicing it wholeheartedly. At the same time, acknowledge that others may hold different viewpoints that seem equally valid to them. While you may express your perspective with clarity, you must not invalidate the perspectives of others. True neutrality, as taught by Anekanta, does not mean straddling both views to avoid conflict. It means evaluating all perspectives openly, without prejudice, and accepting the truth that emerges through fair inquiry.

For instance, whether you perform Pratikraman on Sunday or Monday is secondary to the sincerity and purpose behind the act. If, however, you believe that others observing it on a different day are wrong, then even your 'correct' practice becomes flawed. Similarly, if Sunday observers rigidly assert the supremacy of their practice, and Monday observers do the same, the path of Anekanta urges you to understand the reasoning behind both. Accepting both as equally valid without examination is not neutrality — it is complacency. Neutrality lies in the willingness to investigate first, and only then to conclude.

Many fear that examining multiple viewpoints may lead to attachment (Raag) or aversion (Dvesh). But letting this fear stop you may lead to complacency and thoughtlessness. Anekanta does not promote passivity; it encourages deep, bias-free inquiry. Just as a teacher evaluates exam answers based solely on correctness —

without attachment or aversion — we, too, must learn to assess perspectives with clarity and objectivity.

Never fall into the trap of saying "everything is correct" without analysis — that is ignorance. Instead, before you accept or reject any idea, ensure that your understanding is born of reflection, not of reaction.

10 Transformative Changes Brought by Anekanta

Anekanta is not just a doctrine — it is a transformative force on the spiritual path. It silently reshapes your thinking, interactions, and inner world. Here are ten powerful changes that unfold through the right understanding and application of Anekanta:

1. *Freedom from Conflict*

Anekanta distances you from the urge to argue or prove others wrong. When you believe something to be true, you express it with calm conviction and step back. If questions arise from genuine curiosity, you respond. However, if it's merely an argument in disguise, you gracefully withdraw — even if misunderstood as lacking answers. This fosters harmony, reduces animosity, and helps communities remain united.

2. *Release from Self-Praise*

Self-praise can be toxic. Anekanta removes this poison by teaching you to appreciate virtues wherever they exist — whether in your group (Swapaksha) or outside it (Parapaksha). You no longer believe that all goodness lies solely within your tradition.

3. *Freedom from Criticizing Others*

Anekanta dissolves the habit of dismissing others' views simply because they differ from yours. It cultivates the ability to acknowledge truth even in opposing perspectives. Criticism fades, and when something truly is flawed, it is addressed out without condemnation — critique is directed at the action or idea, not the person.

As *Upadhyay Shri Yashovijayji* explains in the *Sajjhaya* on *Paraparivad Papasthanak*, the scriptures critique actions, not individuals — "Lodhiyaputra did this," or "Kuchikarna acted wrongly." We must learn to reject sin, not the person who perform it.

4. *End of Stubbornness* (Kadagraha)

When both self-glorification and criticism of others reduce, so does stubborn attachment to fixed views. Kadagraha refers accepting truth without understanding its context. Anekanta transforms this into Sadagraha — truth upheld with perspective and reasoning.

5. *Intellectual Openness*

Without Anekanta, we become like frogs in a well-limited and narrow. A closed mind starts to rot, and its toxicity spreads. Anekanta opens the intellect, broadens your vision, and elevates your thinking. Just as climbing a mountain expands your horizon, Anekanta lifts you to a higher vantage point of understanding.

6. *Detachment from Opinions*

You can have faith in a belief, but attachment to it is unnecessary. Often, we hesitate to withdraw a viewpoint fearing damage to our image. Anekanta gives you the courage to let go — freeing you from ego-based attachment to opinions.

This spirit of detachment shaped our 2,500-year-old Jain tradition. Our enlightened ancestors gave up even cherished views for the greater good of Shasan. Tirthankar Mahavira himself taught that one must not even be attached to Jainism, let alone to individual opinions within it.

In a dialogue, Gautamswami asked, "Can I say only those who follow Jainism attain liberation?"

Mahavira responded, “No, Gautam. Dharma is a value, not a sect. One may reach liberation through non-violence, truth, and contentment — these values are not confined to any sect. You may say that Arihants have best articulated how to live these values, but do not claim exclusivity.”

Such non-attachment to even the highest ideals is the very essence of Anekanta.

7. Cultivation of Harmony

As attachment to personal views fades, harmony emerges. Anekanta fosters alignment and mutual respect. Just as merging two firms is harder than splitting one, uniting communities is far more complex than dividing them. Anekanta nurtures the mindset needed for this higher task of integration.

8. Expansion in Depth and Breadth

Anekanta uniquely allows truth to expand in both directions — depth and breadth. Most traditions sacrifice one for the other. Jain philosophy, through Anekanta, balances both. Like water in a glass (deep) and on a plate (wide), truth becomes both profound and vast.

9. *Inner Calm and Peace*

When these qualities manifest, a deep tranquillity follows. A person free of ego, open-minded, detached from opinions, and rooted in perspective-based understanding becomes naturally calm and centred.

10. *Clarity of the Goal* (Sadhya)

Finally, Anekanta sharpens your understanding of the spiritual goal. Often, conflicts arise over the means (Sadhana) because the goal itself is unclear. Once the *Sadhya* is defined, tools become flexible. Anekanta helps you see the difference and stay focused on liberation, not merely on the rituals.

Anekanta: The Lens for Right Engagement and Respect

Shri Haribhadrasuriji Maharaj insightfully observed:

"When a person comes into contact with worldly objects, a deluded mind (Mithyatvi) asks, 'Can this object bring me happiness?' In contrast, a right-seeing mind (Samyaktvi) asks, 'Is this object helpful in attaining liberation (Moksha)?'"

Anekanta as a Guiding Tool

The most effective tool for engaging with people, beliefs, and objects is Anekanta. When encountering any object or person, Anekanta encourages us to ask a fundamental question:

"Is this helpful in my journey toward Moksha?"

This simple shift in inquiry reduces the chances of developing attachment (Raag) or aversion (Dvesh). And even if such emotions arise, they are of a constructive nature:

If attachment arises toward something that furthers your spiritual path, it is purposeful and dissolves easily. If aversion arises toward something obstructive to liberation, it is likewise easier to release.

Cultivating Respect through Anekanta

In families and communities where beliefs differ, peaceful worship and coexistence are entirely possible through Anekanta. We must approach others with patience and humility, gently inspiring them with the message: "This is the path I believe leads to truth."

But if they do not understand or agree, we must avoid conflict, unless a belief system causes deep harm to spiritual values.

Respect is a core principle. Just as you respect your own path, you must learn to extend that same respect to others. Even with inanimate objects, Jain philosophy insists on reverence. For example, if you see an object in your way, the right way is to lift and set it aside — not kick it with your foot. Why?

Because it's not about merely moving the object—it's about your attitude toward it.

If we disrespect objects today, tomorrow we may do the same to people. Disrespect becomes a Sanskar (a deep-rooted habit). That's why Jainism urges us to cultivate universal respect for — people, objects, and beliefs alike.

Discerning Without Condemning

This doesn't mean all actions are to be respected.

For example, slaughtering goats on Bakri Eid is a practice that should be questioned and prevented due to its violent nature.

However, the intention behind the act — devotion, offering to God, and a spirit of charity —deserves acknowledgment and respect.

Anekanta does not advocate for blind tolerance. Instead, it teaches us to carefully examine each belief or practice and determine:

- What is the value behind it?
- Which part deserves respect?
- Which part requires transformation?

Through this lens, we move from indiscriminate opposition to compassionate understanding.

The Seven Pillars of the Shasan and the Role of Anekanta

The foundation of a spiritual system (Shasan) is rooted in **Purnata** (completeness). Only when a Tirthankar attains Kevalgyan (absolute knowledge) and Kevaldarshan (absolute perception) in every dimension does such a system come into existence.

Being born into a religious tradition is a privilege earned through **Punya** (virtue). It is the result from meritorious actions in past lives that granting one the opportunity to follow the path of liberation.

Comprehending the depth of the Shasan requires intellect and insight. It demands **Pratibha** (intellectual brilliance/wisdom) and Antahsphurana (inner intuition).

Serving the Shasan cannot be done passively; it requires sincere **Parishrama** (effort and hard work).

To propagate the teachings of the Shasan and inspire others, one must act with **Prem** (love). Without love, the spirit of the Shasan cannot touch the hearts of others.

To practice the Shasan's teachings, one needs **Prasannata** (conflict-free mind/joy). Only then can spiritual practice be pursued joyfully.

To realize the ultimate goal of the Shasan, one must cultivate **Pavitrata** (purity), which naturally leads to liberation.

These seven pillars — completeness, virtue, wisdom, effort, love, joy, and purity — must be consciously cultivated in life.

No.	Aspect of Shasan	Spiritual Function	Core Virtue	Refined Understanding
1	Establishment	Rooting	**Completeness**	The establishment of the Shasan is rooted in the completeness of absolute knowledge.
2	Attainment	Entry	**Virtue**	Entry into the Shasan is attained through the merit of past virtuous deeds.

No.	Aspect of Shasan	Spiritual Function	Core Virtue	Refined Understanding
3	Understanding	Compre-hension	**Wisdom**	True understanding of the Shasan arises from intellectual clarity and inner insight.
4	Service	Action	**Effort**	Serving the Shasan requires sincere and sustained effort.
5	Promotion	Trans-mission	**Love**	The teachings of the Shasan can only be spread through genuine love and compassion.
6	Adoration	Devotion	**Joy**	Joyful and peaceful adoration brings spiritual fulfillment within the Shasan.
7	Fulfilment	Realization	**Purity**	The fulfilment of the Shasan's ultimate goal depends on inner purity and sincerity.

Anekanta: The Embodiment of the Seven Pillars

Anekanta embodies all seven virtues into our lives, guiding us toward absolute truth and fostering completeness. As you reflect deeply through Anekanta, you engage in Tapasya (spiritual austerity) that generates Punya.

Anekanta opens the doors of the mind, enhancing Pratibha (intellect). It drives you to work sincerely. It fosters harmony and dialogue — through which love blossoms. One who seeks balance and avoids disputes becomes naturally peaceful and joyous. Anekanta brings joy.

Further, Anekanta leads to purity. As the truth becomes evident, it begins to shape your conduct. The Tirthankar teaches that one cannot fully know the truth and fail to live by it. Samyak Gyan (right knowledge) inevitably transforms into Samyak Charitra (right conduct).

Thus, Anekanta should not remain a philosophical idea. It must permeate our spiritual, practical, interpersonal, and global lives. It offers not only self-realization, but also a solution to many global conflicts. Unfortunately, the profound power of Anekanta has not been adequately presented to the world.

The greatest contribution of Jainism is not just Ahinsa (non-violence), but also Anekanta. While non-violence has existed in various forms globally, Anekanta is a unique offering with the potential to resolve the world's deepest challenges.

Presenting Anekanta to the World

When someone asks about Jainism, we often present a list of dos and don'ts. Rarely do we introduce Anekanta. As a result, the true grandeur of Jainism remains hidden.

When we say, "Jainam Jayati Shasanam," it does not mean other faiths are inferior. It means truth prevails to the extent that a system embraces it. Jain Shasan is not an isolated tradition; it is an integration of all valid perspectives. It is like declaring, "The 14 Rajloks prevail" — a statement that encompasses everything.

The real essence of "Jainam Jayati Shasanam" is: Anekanta prevails.

Every religion consists of three parts: Ideals, Conduct and Principles

In Jainism:

- Ideals are tested through Kash (evaluation)

- Conduct through Chhed (dissection)
- Principles through Taap (refinement)

Just as gold is tested by touchstone, cutting, and fire — so too must religion be tested. Jainism welcomes this process.

Most doctrines claim, "We alone are right." But Jainism says: anyone who practices values like truth and non-violence can attain liberation, regardless of religious label. This unique inclusivity is the heart of Anekanta.

While other religions may offer ideals and conduct, only Jainism elevates Anekanta to its highest expression. That is why Jainam Jayati Shasanam.

The Fine Line Between Steadfastness and Rigidity

We must hold firm to our truths — that is Nishtha (steadfastness). But rigidity arises when we reject other perspectives without examination. If another view is found to be 100% incorrect after honest reflection, it may be discarded — but not out of arrogance or dismissal.

Steadfastness means embracing our truth; rigidity implies opposing others.

We claim to follow the Arihants, yet often forget their core values. Consider the story:

A group offered lavish devotion to their king — gems, pearls, dedicated service — but made one request: "We shall do everything for you, except follow your commands." What value does such devotion hold?

In the same way, we often offer ritualistic devotion to the Arihants but ignore their teachings. This renders our devotion hollow.

Let us not become absorbed in ideals while forgetting the principles they were meant to illuminate. The Arihants gave us both — let us honour both with equal sincerity.

Living Anekanta: From Insight to Integration

Anekantvad is not meant to sit silently in books or remain confined to debates on doctrine. It is a living truth — one that must breathe through our thoughts, words, and actions. It challenges us to go beyond passive tolerance or ritual repetition and instead enter a state of dynamic awareness. In a world echoing with division, Anekanta whispers the wisdom of wholeness.

This is not an invitation to become indecisive. Nor does it mean we must accept everything as equal. Anekant does not dilute truth — it deepens it. It teaches us to hold our convictions with humility, to stand rooted in our insights without invalidating the journey of others. It transforms our inner posture from arrogance to inquiry, from defensiveness to discernment.

When Anekanta seeps into our gaze, we stop asking, "Who is right?" and start asking, "What is true?" We no longer see disagreement as a threat, but as a doorway to dialogue.

We begin to speak less from ego, and more from understanding. And slowly, almost quietly, the world around us begins to change — not because we forced it to, but because we changed how we see.

This is the silent strength of Anekanta: It does not shout, but it transforms. It does not conquer, but it connects. It does not divide, but it clarifies. It shows us that truth is not a wall to defend — it is a sky to open into.

Let us not merely study Anekantvad. Let us *live* it — in our homes, our conversations, our communities, and our hearts. For in doing so, we do not just understand Jainism — we embody its very soul.

Discourse 04

Reflection questions

1. Do I follow religious or spiritual practices out of tradition, or have I consciously chosen and understood them?
2. How can I honour my own beliefs without invalidating the perspectives of others?
3. In what ways can I balance faith and critical inquiry in my spiritual journey?

Discourse 04

Short practices

Philosophical:

List 3 spiritual or religious practices you follow. For each, write:

- Do I understand why I follow this?
- Is it a matter of faith or reason? Reflect: Can I deepen its meaning by exploring its philosophical roots?

Journal:

Identify where in your life you're most rigid. What might flexibility look like there?

Behavioural:

For one day, avoid using absolute language (always, never, everyone, no one).

Meditation:

Breathe deeply and affirm – 'All truths contribute to the whole.'

Image description

This image powerfully illustrates the transformative essence of Anekanta — the Jain doctrine of pluralism — without using any text. At its centre is a human silhouette, symbolizing introspection and inner awakening. Surrounding the figure are swirling layers of light and colour, representing the diverse perspectives and multifaceted nature of truth. The luminous network signifies the sharpening of intellect and deepened understanding that Anekanta fosters. Each layer reflects the peeling away of biases and rigid beliefs, leading the mind toward flexibility and expanded awareness. The image as a whole embodies the journey from fragmented perception to wholeness, guided by the quiet strength of Anekanta.

Discourse 05

ANEKANTA: A CATALYST FOR UNFOLDING INNER POTENTIAL

Introduction:

Anekanta, the cornerstone of Jain philosophy, is not merely a doctrine of multiple perspectives — it is a powerful tool for inner transformation. By acknowledging the relativity of truth, Anekanta trains the mind to move beyond rigid thinking while cultivates intellectual humility. This flexibility allows us to embrace diverse viewpoints, break free from limiting beliefs, and tap into our deeper potential. It sharpens our reasoning, broadens our perception, and enhances our emotional maturity. As we develop the ability to see reality in layered dimensions, we begin shedding biases that hinder personal growth. Thus, Anekanta does more than shape our worldview — it serves us a catalyst for the conscious evolution of the self. In every moment of introspection, it gently nudges us toward wholeness.

Key theme:

Anekanta is not only a tool for understanding others — it is a powerful method for inner growth. This discourse illustrates how pluralistic thinking sharpens our perception, dissolves biases, and awakens dormant possibilities within. It teaches us that by embracing complexity, we cultivate depth.

The Transformative Power of Anekanta

Upadan refers to the soul's capacity for purification and spiritual evolution. However, for this transformation to take place, the presence of a **Nimitt** (an external catalyst or condition) is essential. Throughout history, countless Upadans (souls) have wandered aimlessly, unable to realize their potential simply because a suitable Nimitt was absent. This reflection is an attempt to identify and acknowledge such a Nimitt for our own development.

When we reflect upon the life of Damayanti Mahasati, we are awestruck by her resilience and inner strength. Abandoned in the forest by King Nala, she wandered alone and eventually reached an ashram of 500 ascetics. Despite laking scriptural mastery of the 11 Angas or the profound knowledge of a Purvadhar, Damayanti — through her unwavering faith and deep understanding of Anekanta — engaged in meaningful dialogue and gradually led these ascetics toward Samyaktva (right perception), ultimately inspiring them to accept Diksha. This was not a miracle — it was the silent strength of Anekanta. If such transformation was possible for her, it is equally possible for us if we embody the same devotion and insight.

Upadhyay Shri Yashovijayji beautifully explains that all Nayas (viewpoints) are like children — and

Anekanta, like a mother, does not discriminate. It neither ranks nor invalidates any Naya. However, we often fall into the trap of considering Vyavahar Naya as inferior and Nishchay Naya as superior. In truth, both have their place and purpose. Vyavahar Naya leads knowledge toward Rati (attraction and faith), while Nishchay Naya channels knowledge into Virati (renunciation). At the fourth Gunasthan, knowledge breeds faith; at the sixth, it cultivates conduct. There is no superiority or inferiority — only contextual relevance.

One who understands the equanimity of all philosophies, applies Syadvad as the lens to keep Moksha as the goal, is truly a scriptural knower in Jainism.

Merely imparting scriptural knowledge is not enough. One must embody neutrality (Madhyasthata) grounded in Syadvad. Even a single principle, when deeply internalized with neutrality, holds more value than an encyclopedic memory devoid of balanced perspective. Without neutrality, even profound scriptural mastery fails to inspire upliftment.

The Tirthankar clearly states: even if a Mithyatvi (deluded soul) masters the knowledge of the nine Purvas, it is of no spiritual value. Why? Because:

There is no faith in Moksha.

There is no understanding of Syadvad.

Hence, no matter how vast one's knowledge may be, without Syadvad, it becomes spiritually ineffective. The purpose of knowledge is to facilitate transformation, which is only possible through balanced perception.

As *Upadhyay Shri Yashovijayji* aptly wrote:

"Syadvad poorna jo jaane,

Nayagarbhit jas vaacha,

Gun-Paryay-Dravya jo jaane,

So hi Jain hai saacha..."

He who understands Syadvad in its fullness and speaks from a perspective enriched by all viewpoints — who knows the interplay of qualities, modes, and substance — he alone is truly a Jain.

To merely label oneself as a Jain is not enough. If the core principle of Anekanta is absent, even fundamental truths remain fragmented. Without Anekanta, faith becomes fragile — vulnerable to collapse in the face of adversity. But faith rooted in knowledge is unshakable. Our scriptures say that Samyaktva (right faith) can endure for

66 Sagaropamas (a long time) – how? Because it stands on the solid foundation of knowledge and clarity.

Syadvad instills reverence within us. The way the Tirthankar has explained every truth with such nuance is astonishing. This reverence itself becomes the cornerstone of faith. When rooted in this depth, no external situation can shake it.

Anekanta teaches us that every situation carries the potential for transformation. When joy comes, we don't become arrogant. When sorrow arrives, we don't lose hope. With Anekanta, we stay grounded in every circumstance, maintaining awareness, balance, and openness.

The Four Dimensions of Existence

The existence of any entity can be understood through four fundamental aspects: Dravya (Matter), Kshetra (Space), Kaal (Time), and Bhaav / Paryaya (State)

Any object or being can be described as:

"At this time, in this space, this matter exists in this particular state."

Example: If you are wearing a gold chain, it can be expressed as: "At this moment (Kaal), the gold (Dravya) exists as a chain (Paryaya) around my neck (Kshetra)."

Explanation of the Four Aspects:

- Dravya (Matter) – The original substance or base material. Example: Gold
- Kshetra (Space) – The specific location of the object. Example: Around my neck
- Kaal (Time) – The time frame in which the object exists. Example: The present moment
- Bhaav / Paryaya (State) – The condition or form in which the matter exists. Example: As a chain

If even one of these four aspects is altered, the entity's current state of existence is no longer the same.

Illustrative Example:

Let's consider the statement:

"At this moment, a plastic pen is in my hand."

Here, Plastic = Dravya (Matter), Pen = Paryaya (State), My hand = Kshetra (Space), This moment = Kaal (Time).

Changing one aspect at a time:

- Kaal (Time): If we change "this moment" to "five minutes ago," the pen may not have been in my hand.

- Kshetra (Space): If we change "my hand" to "your hand," the pen is no longer in the original space.
- Dravya (Matter): If we replace "plastic" with "gold," the object becomes a different pen altogether.
- Paryaya (State): If we replace "pen" with "clip," then the object in hand is no longer a pen.

The Nature of Change and Impermanence

From the moment something is born, it begins to transform and eventually perish.

The time lapse between birth and death is just a moment – the gradual dissipation of Ayushya Karma particles leads to death.

Every second, our physical and internal states change — yet we tend to notice only major changes. This emphasizes the impermanence and relativity of existence.

From Relativity to Saptabhangi

Since an object's existence is relative to its matter, space, time, and state, absolute statements about anything are inherently flawed.

This relativity is captured in the Jain doctrine of Saptabhangi – the seven-fold logic.

What is Saptabhangi?

Saptabhangi explains how a particular attribute (Dharma) exists — or doesn't — within an entity (Dharmi), from seven logical perspectives.

Rules of Saptabhangi:

In all seven Bhanga (perspectives), the Dharmi (subject) and Dharma (attribute) remain the same.

The variation arises purely due to a change in context (Apeksha).

The first perspective asserts "Yes" (affirmation), and the second states "No" (negation), laying the foundation for the rest.

Perspective (Bhanga)	Meaning
1. Syad Asti	In some respect, it exists.
2. Syad Nasti	In some respect, it does not exist.
3. Syad Asti Nasti	In some respect, it exists and does not exist.
4. Syad Avaktavya	In some respect, it is indescribable.
5. Syad Asti Avaktavya	In some respect, it exists and is indescribable.

6. Syad Nasti Avaktavya	In some respect, it does not exist and is indescribable.
7. Syad Asti Nasti Avaktavya	In some respect, it exists, does not exist, and is indescribable.

Example

Bhanga	Dharmi (Entity)	Dharma (Attribute)	Apeksha (Perspective)	Outcome
1	Pen	Blackness	Viewing the cap portion	**Yes**
2	Pen	Blackness	Viewing the rest of the pen (excluding cap)	**No**

Understanding Saptabhangi Through Examples

Let us understand Saptabhangi (the sevenfold predication) with the help of a practical example.

If I take a pen as the Dharmi (entity) and blackness as the Dharma (attribute), and you ask me: “Is there blackness in the pen?”

Ordinarily, one might answer "yes" or "no" based on general observation. But through the lens of Saptabhangi:

First Bhanga: Yes, from the perspective of the cap, the pen has blackness.

Here, pen is the Dharmi, blackness is the Dharma, and the cap is the Apeksha (perspective).

Second Bhanga: No, from the perspective of the rest of the pen's body (excluding the cap), there is no blackness.

Let us see another example:

"Is this blanket yellow?"

Yes, from the perspective of the parts excluding the design, the blanket is yellow. No, from the perspective of the design, it is not yellow.

Thus, two contradictory perspectives — Bhanga — arise.

The Universality of Relative Existence

Take any entity (Dharmi) in the world and any of its infinite attributes (Dharmas), and you will always find at least these first two perspectives:

From one Apeksha (viewpoint), the attribute exists in the entity.

From another Apeksha, the same attribute does not exist in the same entity.

A Third Example: The Omniscient Soul

"Does a Kevalgyani (omniscient being) possess Kevalgyan (omniscience)?"

Yes, from the perspective of their current enlightened state, they possess Kevalgyan.

No, from the perspective of their earlier, non-enlightened (Chhadmastha) state, they did not possess it.

Hence, even in a single soul (Atma), both statements are valid under different perspectives. These contradictory but valid answers are foundational to Relative Existence (Sapeksha Astitva).

For example:

The soul is eternal from the perspective of substance (Dravya),

But not eternal from the perspective of form (Paryaya).

The Third Bhanga: Holistic View

Now, if I ask: "Not just from the cap or body separately — is the entire pen black?"

Then: From a holistic perspective, the pen is both black and not black. But this cannot be expressed in a single word. Even saying "is and is not" involves two terms.

To express this indivisible truth in one word is impossible, because two contradictory conditions are being stated together.

The Inexpressible Bhanga – Shunya or Avaktavya

When such holistic, non-divisible perspectives arise: The only possible expression is Shunya (zero) or Avaktavya (inexpressible).

This doesn't mean that nothing exists — it simply means it cannot be spoken in definite terms, though it can be understood.

Thus, the third Bhanga becomes the bridge between dual expression and inexpressible understanding — an essential part of the profound logic of Saptabhangi.

Applying Saptabhangi to the Concept of Humanness

It is common to say, "We are all human." However, the more accurate expression is: "Currently, my soul (Dravya) is in the form (Paryaya) of a human."

Now, if someone asks, "Are you human?", we can explore this question through the lens of Saptabhangi (the sevenfold predication).

First, let us identify:

- Dharmi (Entity): The soul
- Dharma (Attribute): Humanness
- Apeksha (Perspective): Varies depending on the timeframe or condition

Saptabhangi Breakdown

Bhanga	Dharmi (Entity)	Dharma (Attribute)	Apeksha (Perspective)	Outcome
1	Soul	Humanness	This life	Yes
2	Soul	Humanness	Next life	No
3	Soul	Humanness	Totality (this + next life, together)	Inexpressible (Avaktavya)
4	Soul	Humanness	This life + Next life	Yes + No
5	Soul	Humanness	This life + Totality	Yes + Inexpressible
6	Soul	Humanness	Next life + Totality	No + Inexpressible
7	Soul	Humanness	This life + Next life + Totality	Yes + No + Inexpressible

Clarifying the Terms:

- **Yes**: Humanness exists under that specific perspective
- **No**: Humanness does not exist under that perspective
- **Avaktavya (Inexpressible)**: The condition can be understood but not expressed in one word
- **Totality (Samagrata)**: A non-fragmented, holistic view considering all timeframes together

Fundamental Framework of Saptabhangi

Saptabhangi is built on three core Bhangas (stances):

- It exists (under a certain condition)
- It does not exist (under another condition)
- It is inexpressible (when viewed from totality)

From these, the remaining four composite Bhangas are derived: (From the table on page 151)

- 1 + 2 = Bhanga 4
- 1 + 3 = Bhanga 5
- 2 + 3 = Bhanga 6

- 1 + 2 + 3 = Bhanga 7

Interpreting the Sevenfold Response:

- My soul, from the perspective of this life, possesses humanness.
- My soul, in the context of the next life, does not possess humanness.
- When viewed from totality, the truth is Avaktavya – I understand, but cannot express it in one word.
- Considering this life and next life separately: humanness both exists and does not exist.
- This life + totality: Humanness exists and is also inexpressible.
- Next life + totality: Humanness does not exist and is inexpressible.
- Considering all three perspectives together: Humanness exists, does not exist, and is inexpressible.

Constructing Saptabhangi with Divinity (Devatva) as the Attribute

Now, suppose we replace the attribute Humanness with Divinity (Devatva). In that case, the Saptabhangi construction will change accordingly. By rule, the first Bhanga must always affirm the attribute (answer: Yes) from a valid perspective.

Saptabhangi Table: Soul as Dharmi and Divinity as Dharma

Bhanga	Dharmi (Entity)	Dharma (Attribute)	Apeksha (Perspective)	Outcome
1	Soul	Divinity	Next life	Yes
2	Soul	Divinity	This life	No
3	Soul	Divinity	Totality (this + next life combined)	Inexpressible (Avaktavya)
4	Soul	Divinity	Next life + This life	Yes + No
5	Soul	Divinity	Next life + Totality	Yes + Inexpressible
6	Soul	Divinity	This life + Totality	No + Inexpressible
7	Soul	Divinity	Next life + This life + Totality	Yes + No + Inexpressible

Key Clarifications:

The perspectives (Apeksha) shift because the attribute has changed. When dealing with Humanness, the first Bhanga focused on this life; with Divinity, the first Bhanga focuses on next life.

This structure is not random – it follows predefined rules that guide the systematic construction of Saptabhangi.

How to Construct Saptabhangi for Any Attribute:

Identify the Dharmi: The entity or substance (e.g., soul, pot, pen).

Choose the Dharma: One specific attribute out of its infinite attributes.

Define the Perspectives (Apeksha):

- Where the Dharma exists in the Dharmi.
- Where the Dharma does not exist in the Dharmi.

Totality (Samagrata): A non-separative view of both perspectives.

Set up a table with five columns:

Column 1: Bhanga number (1 to 7)

Column 2: Dharmi (remains same throughout)

Column 3: Dharma (attribute under consideration)

Column 4: Apeksha (perspective)

- Row 1: Perspective where Dharma exists
- Row 2: Perspective where Dharma does not exist
- Row 3: Totality
- Rows 4–7: Logical combinations → 1+2, 1+3, 2+3, 1+2+3

Column 5: Outcome (Yes / No / Inexpressible and their combinations)

The outcomes will always be one of these seven:

- Yes
- No
- Inexpressible
- Yes + No
- Yes + Inexpressible
- No + Inexpressible
- Yes + No + Inexpressible

Use of "Syad" in Classical Sanskrit Construction:

In Sanskrit texts, the word 'Syad' (स्याद्) is used instead of explicitly stating the perspectives.

Syad signifies "from a certain perspective."

The term implies a specific Apeksha without always naming it.

This is why Saptabhangi, though technically a subset of Anekanta, is historically associated with the term Syadvad.

Syad = perspective, Vad = to express or speak.

So Syadvad means "to speak with perspective in mind."

Though Syadvad is often used to represent the entire doctrine of Anekanta, it primarily pertains to the sevenfold predication rooted in perspective-based reasoning.

Reflections on the Depth and Utility of Anekanta and Saptabhangi

A Samyaktvi Jeev (a soul with right faith) may not explicitly use the word Syad every time they speak. However, because the impression of Syad is deeply embedded in their consciousness, every thought or expression they offer inherently carries the essence of Syadvad — the perspective-based view of reality.

The scriptures pose a profound question: If someone takes Diksha (spiritual initiation) at the age of 8 in Mahavideha Kshetra and lives for a crore Purva (an immensely long span of time), how should that life be spent?

The answer: Immerse the mind in constant contemplation of Anekanta. This contemplation, pursued over countless years, leads to moment-to-moment Nirjara — the continuous shedding of karmic matter.

Clarifications and Applications

Q: How can one object possess infinite attributes?

A: According to Jain scriptures, infinity is beyond the full grasp of a deluded (Mithyatvi) or limited soul (Chhadmastha). The notion that a single entity possesses infinite attributes cannot be comprehended fully through limited intellect. To approach this truth, the scriptures provide logical reasoning and illustrative analogies for deeper study and contemplation.

Q: Where is Saptabhangi used?

A: While Saptabhangi is deeply rooted in philosophical inquiry, it also holds immense value in practical and religious life.

By applying the lens of Saptabhangi to various situations, the mind becomes peaceful, and conflicting views can be harmonized through contextual understanding (Apeksha).

It clarifies how a change in perspective naturally leads to a change in conclusion, which helps dissolve attachment or aversion to one-sided thinking.

Consequently, both joy and sorrow are understood within their relative contexts, fostering inner equanimity.

Cultivating the Inner Eye of Anekanta

Anekanta is not just a way to understand others — it is a profound method of understanding the self. When we see that truth has many facets, we stop clinging to absolutes and begin listening more deeply — to others, to life, and to our own evolving awareness.

The doctrines of Syadvad and Saptabhangi are not abstract theories; they are mirrors that reveal our inner biases and guide us toward balance. They teach us how to think, not what to think. Through them, Anekanta becomes a lifelong meditation — on humility, clarity, and wholeness.

When we begin to see reality in layers — as Dravya, Guna, Paryaya, Kaal, Kshetra, and Bhaav — a new kind of wisdom awakens. This wisdom does not divide; it integrates. It does not react; it reflects. It does not conquer; it transforms.

In a divided world, Anekanta offers a rare gift:

A mind that listens, a heart that understands, and a soul that evolves.

Let this understanding not remain in words. Let it become the way we see, speak, and live.

Discourse 05

Reflection questions

1. What personal biases am I ready to shed in order to grow intellectually and spiritually?
2. Who or what has been a Nimitt (catalyst) in my life that helped me recognize deeper truths?
3. How can I become a Nimitt for others by embodying Anekanta in my thoughts, words, and actions?

Discourse 05

Short practices

Philosophical:

Recall one person or situation that helped you grow mentally or spiritually. Write:

- What was the trigger?
- What inner potential did it reveal? Now, set one small intention today to be a Nimitt (catalyst) for someone else's growth.

Journal:

List three ways your potential has been limited by one-sided views (from self or others).

Behavioural:

Choose one area of personal growth and explore it from multiple viewpoints (spiritual, emotional, rational).

Meditation:

Imagine peeling layers of identity, discovering deeper truths beyond each one.

Conclusion

Living Anekanta in a Fragmented World

As we arrive at the conclusion of **Pluralism with Purpose: Understanding Anekanta**, one truth stands out with crystal clarity: Anekanta is not just a doctrine for debate halls or scriptural study — it is a way of living that the modern world desperately needs. In times where social, political, and spiritual polarities are deepening, Anekanta offers a path that leads us away from conflict and toward coexistence.

The true power of Anekanta lies in its ability to dissolve the ego's desire to be absolutely right. It trains us to listen without judgment, speak without dominance, and think without rigidity. It invites us to see beyond the surface — to recognize that every person, idea, or situation carries multiple layers of truth, some visible and some yet to unfold.

In our homes, Anekanta nurtures empathy in relationships. It teaches us that understanding is more important than agreement, and that different opinions do not mean disloyalty or disrespect. At work, Anekanta enables creative problem-solving by opening our minds to multiple viewpoints. In society, it becomes a force of peace, urging us to replace intolerance with inquiry and prejudice with perspective.

Spiritually, Anekanta leads us toward a humility of the highest order — the humility that says, "What I know is only one side of truth; let me remain open to more." This spiritual openness fosters deeper self-awareness, inner stillness, and true non-violence, not just in actions but also in thoughts.

By practicing Anekanta, we begin to experience a quiet transformation. Our judgments soften, our thinking expands, and our hearts open to truths we once rejected. We no longer seek to defeat others in conversation — we seek to understand them. And in doing so, we start to understand ourselves.

May this spirit of Anekanta guide your actions, inspire your reflections, and uplift your spiritual journey — not just as an idea to admire, but as a truth to live by.

Part Two

TEACHINGS OF SPECIAL SUBJECTS

Part 2 – Teachings of Special Subjects

Index

1

The Form of Dravya (Matter), Guṇa (Quality), and Paryāya (Form)

Let us begin by exploring one of the foundational concepts of Anekānta — Dravya-Guṇa-Paryāya (Matter-Quality-Form). This discussion is housed within the framework of Dravyānuyoga, one of the four Anuyogas through which Jain scriptural knowledge is systematized. The four Anuyogas are:

- **Dravyānuyoga** – Philosophical exposition
- **Cāraṇānuyoga** – Ethical conduct
- **Dharmakathānuyoga** – Narrative and illustrative stories
- **Gaṇitānuyoga** – Mathematical and cosmological measurements

What is Anuyoga?

The term Anuyoga combines 'Anu' (meaning "after" or "following") and 'Yoga' (meaning "to unite" or "to apply").

Hence, Anuyoga refers to the method of scriptural interpretation rooted in foundational principles (Sūtras). Different scriptures are interpreted through different lenses — some philosophically, some ethically, some mathematically, and some narratively.

Of these, Dravyānuyoga is often the most overlooked. While many may be familiar with Jain stories (Dharmakathānuyoga), cosmological figures like the height of Mount Meru (Gaṇitānuyoga), or rituals such as Sāmāyika and Pūjā (Cāraṇānuyoga), few delve into the rich philosophical core that Dravyānuyoga offers. Yet, learned masters have emphasized that without Dravyānuyoga, the remaining three Anuyogas lack true substance. Only Dravyānuyoga leads to realization of the true Self and Moksha (liberation).

While Dravyānuyoga is a vast and profound subject, our current focus is a small but critical part of it — the doctrine of Anekāntavāda (Pluralism). The more deeply one engages with this principle, the more naturally one is drawn into the heart of Dravyānuyoga.

To begin understanding Dravyānuyoga, we must grasp the triad of Dravya (Matter), Guṇa (Quality), and Paryāya (Form or Modification). These three elements form the essence of all universal truth. Everything in existence falls under one of these three categories.

What is Dravya (Matter)?

1. *Matter is the substratum of qualities.*

Qualities exist only in relation to matter. For example, knowledge is a quality. What is its substratum? The Soul. The white hue of a Sthāpanāji (idol) is a quality — its base is the idol itself. Hence, Dravya is that which holds or sustains qualities.

2. *Matter is that which manifests in different forms (Paryāyas).*

In Jain philosophy, Paryāya denotes any state or modification of a substance. Gold, for instance, can be molded into a ring, melted and reshaped into an earring, and again into a chain or ornament. These are different Paryāyas (forms) of the same Dravya (gold). The underlying gold remains constant — only its forms change. Over 2,500 years ago, Jain philosophy declared that matter in this universe neither increases nor decreases; only its modifications change. Thus, that which takes on various forms without itself being diminished or destroyed is called Dravya.

3. *Matter is that which remains constant across all three tenses – past, present, and future.*

Gold was gold yesterday, is gold today, and will remain gold tomorrow. Even before a ring is crafted, the gold exists; it continues to exist as the ring, and it remains gold even when the ring is destroyed. Matter thus remains unchanged across time, even though its forms may change.

4. That Which is Known Through Its Own Properties

Dravya is that which is known through its inherent qualities. When matter manifests into form, we identify it based on that form. When the soul takes on a human form, it is called a human being. Thus, what is recognized through its attributes is Dravya.

Each of these definitions interrelate. They are provided separately only to facilitate understanding. In essence:

- Dravya is recognized through its attributes.
- Dravya supports Paryāya (forms).
- Dravya remains constant in all three dimensions of time.
- Dravya is the substratum of qualities.

These insights are fundamental to unlocking the philosophical dimensions of Anekānta and the broader canvas of Jain metaphysics.

Types of Dravya: Mūla Dravya and Ādiṣta Dravya

- There are two categories of Dravya (substance/matter):
  1. Mūla Dravya (Fundamental Matter)
- 2. Ādiṣta Dravya (Transformed Matter)

To understand the fundamental, let us first grasp the transformed. The atoms of gold today can become the atoms of a pot tomorrow — because atoms are ever-changing. For example, quantum particles that form milk today may become clarified butter (ghee) tomorrow, then food, then faeces, then soil, then grass, and again return to milk. This endless cycle of transformation continues, yet the quantum particles themselves remain constant.

Some things appear to persist across time but are, in truth, only temporary. Consider a pot: suppose it lasts 20 years before breaking. In that span, it may change appearance, be painted, filled with fragrances, or show signs of aging. These are various forms (Paryāya) of the pot, yet they do not alter the fundamental substance — clay. Once broken, we realize that the pot was never the Dravya; it was merely a form (Paryāya) of clay, the actual Dravya.

We tend to mistake long-lasting forms for substances. But in reality, the pot is not Dravya; it is a durable Paryāya, and the term Ādiṣta Dravya refers to such forms mistakenly regarded as substance. Ādiṣta means "designated" — used for practical reference though not fundamentally real.

The true Mūla Dravya is the indivisible quantum particle, while all recognizable forms — like pot, human, tree — are Ādiṣta Dravya, sustained by a collection of constantly changing Paryāya.

Understanding Guṇa (Quality) and Paryāya (Form)

Guṇa and Paryāya must be understood together. Consider this: your awareness of a Sthāpanāji (idol) arises when it enters your attention. Yet your soul has always possessed the potential for knowledge. This implies that knowledge is eternal, even though specific knowledge (like identifying a Sthāpanāji) may come and go.

Guṇa refers to eternal, inherent qualities (Sahabhāvi) — like knowledge in the soul or colour in a particle. Paryāya refers to temporary, changing states (Kramabhāvi) — like being a child, adult, or elder.

So, while colour as a concept is natural to particles, red, white, or black are changeable forms. A particle may lack red, but not colour entirely. Thus:

- Natural, unchanging characteristics = Guṇa
- Temporary, changing characteristics = Paryāya

Even the soul must always exist in some form — it cannot exist formlessly. But its embodiment as a human is a Paryāya, not a Guṇa.

Two Types of Paryāya

There are two types of Paryāya:

1. **Artha-Paryāya** (Attributive, fast-changing)

2. **Vyanjana-Paryāya** (Gross, aggregated)

Artha-Paryāya changes moment by moment and is imperceptible to ordinary minds. Vyanjana-Paryāya is the accumulation of many subtle changes, visible as a gross shift. For instance, a child grows daily (Artha-Paryāya), but a distant relative notices the change after months (Vyanjana-Paryāya).

We typically notice only Vyanjana-Paryāya and mistake it for the only reality. But the truth is that reality changes constantly and subtly. The pot, ring, and person are all results of ongoing, invisible changes in form — each sustained by a more fundamental Dravya.

2

The Relationship of Dravya (Matter), Paryāya (Form), and Padārtha (Object)

The fundamental equation can be articulated as: Dravya (Matter) + Paryāya (Form) = Padārtha (Object). Nimitta Kāraṇa (Instrumental causes) assist the Upādāna Dravya (Material cause) in assuming a specific form. For example, a goldsmith shapes gold into a ring. The gold is the Upādāna Dravya, and the goldsmith is the Nimitta. Their combined effort produces a recognizable object — the ring.

When clay is moulded into a specific form, it becomes a pot. Had it been shaped differently; it could become a pan. The form changes, but the matter (clay) remains the same. This demonstrates that while Paryāya varies, the Upādāna Dravya remains constant.

Vertical and Horizontal Continuity

The Upādāna Dravya remains over time and is known as Ūrdhvatva Sāmānya (Vertical Continuity). Why this term? Imagine a pot, a pan, and a lamp — all made from the same clay. The pot must cease to exist for the clay to become a pan. The forms don't coexist simultaneously. Visualize this sequence vertically — one after another over time.

Now imagine three pots — one of clay, one of gold, and one of copper — all existing simultaneously, and all having the same shape. This is Tiryak Sāmānya (Horizontal Continuity). It illustrates similarity of form across different matters at the same time, while vertical continuity reflects similarity of matter across time.

Eternal Matter, Impermanent Form

An object (Padārtha) is eternal from the perspective of Dravya, but impermanent from the perspective of Paryāya.

- Dravya is stable due to Dhrauvya (permanence).
- Paryāya is impermanent due to constant Utpad (origination) and Vināsh (destruction).

When clay exists in raw form, the pot already exists within it — not as a form, but as matter. Similarly, Marichi, in his third birth, is referred to as a Dravya Tirthankara, even though the Paryāya of Tirthankara has not yet manifested. The potential exists.

Thus, even without the visible form, the Upādāna Dravya validates the existence of the object. For example:

- Clay → Dravya Ghado (Pot-in-substance)
- Soul → Dravya Tirthankara (Tirthankara-in-substance)

The Triple Process of All Substances

At every single moment, all substances undergo:

1. Utpad (Origination)
2. Vināsh (Destruction)
3. Dhrauvya (Stability)

Due to our limited understanding, we perceive only major changes, but subtle transformations are constantly occurring. Scriptures help bridge this perceptual gap.

Scriptural Viewpoint (i = Iti; va = Apeksha)

Each object, in every moment, undergoes all three conditions:

Uppanne i va – In some respect, it is originating.

Vigaye i va – In some respect, it is being destroyed.

Dhruve i va – In some respect, it remains constant.

This triple condition reflects the dynamic but stable nature of Dravya and Paryāya:

Origination and Destruction indicate impermanence (of form). Stability (Dhrauvya) affirms the permanence (of matter).

Thus, every object is a constant interplay of creation, cessation, and continuity, always in flow yet grounded in permanence.

3

General and Distinct Perspectives

When evaluating two objects, ideas, or situations, the Tirthankar advises beginning with this understanding: no two entities are completely identical, nor are they entirely different. If they were completely identical, they would merge into one; if entirely different, they could not coexist within the same universe. Hence, we are taught to nurture two kinds of perspectives — the general, which highlights similarities, and the distinct, which discerns differences.

Whenever confronted with a dilemma, begin by identifying the commonalities between the options. Acknowledge the shared elements, set them aside, and then shift your focus to the differences — examine their nature and implications. This clarity allows balanced judgment and resolves confusion.

Confusion often arises from an inability to assess the degree of truth or falsity in a situation. The inability to discern leads to stagnation. The moment you cultivate the capacity to separate the general from the specific, that very moment confusion begins to dissolve.

Philosophically, general perspective is aligned with observation, while distinct perspective is associated with knowledge. Both are necessary and should coexist. Overemphasis on either — trying to erase differences or exaggerate them — leads to disharmony.

Some people impose similarity on everything, attempting to mold others into their own image, thus erasing individuality. This often creates conflict, as they expect others to do things "their way." On the flip side, others see only differences and fail to recognize underlying unity. Anekantvad teaches balance — acknowledging both similarity and difference.

4

Sat-Asat Karyavad

(The Doctrine of Existence and Non-Existence in Effect)

Anekantvad further reveals that only what inherently exists within a cause can manifest as an effect. If something is not present in the material cause (Upadan Dravya), no amount of effort (Nimitt) can bring it into existence. For instance, no matter how hard you try, you cannot make a pot out of cloth – because a pot is not latent in cloth. It can only be created from clay, which contains the inherent potential for becoming a pot.

This principle is known as Sat-Asat Karyavad – the Doctrine of Existence and Non-Existence in Effect. It asserts that even if something is not visible, it may exist in a latent state within its material cause. Through appropriate effort, it can manifest. Thus, the effect is both existent (Sat) and non-existent (Asat) in its cause – present in potential, absent in form.

Practically, this doctrine encourages wisdom in effort. Often, people feel frustrated when their hard work doesn't yield success. Syadvad teaches us to first assess whether the outcome is even possible, i.e., whether it exists inherently in the material cause. Acting without understanding this leads to unnecessary failure.

For example, some parents push children into fields where the child's inherent aptitude does not lie — a creative child forced into accountancy, or a sensitive soul pushed into medical school. The result? Struggles, stress, and unmet expectations.

Syadvad advises: first examine the nature of the material, recognizc its capacity, and then direct your effort. When action is aligned with potential, success becomes far more likely.

The Tirthankar has recognized in each of us the inherent potential to realize Anekantvad. This realization is our privilege and our path. Let us walk it with faith and resolve, moving even closer to the liberation (Moksha) that lies at its end.

5

Understanding the Seven Nayas (Viewpoints) in Jain Philosophy

What is Naya?

Naya refers to a perspective or a specific lens through which we observe or interpret a thing, idea, or situation. At its core, Naya is a way of thinking—an ideology. When this ideology is expressed in words, those words too are referred to as Naya. Thus, Naya operates at both the conceptual (thought) and practical (behavioural and verbal) levels.

Samgraha Naya – The Collective Viewpoint

This viewpoint focuses on identifying commonalities or shared characteristics. People guided by Samgraha Naya see unity — "A country is a country, whether India or Pakistan." This ideology tends to merge distinctions and highlight universal features across objects or ideas. Since similarities can manifest in countless ways, Samgraha Naya has infinite subtypes.

Vyavahara Naya – The Practical / Differentiating Viewpoint

Opposite to Samgraha Naya, Vyavahara Naya emphasizes differences. A person guided by this viewpoint instinctively identifies distinctions, even between seemingly identical objects. Their behaviour and speech reflect this analytical inclination. Just as similarities have infinite forms, so do differences, making this Naya equally diverse.

Rujusutra Naya – The Present-Focused Viewpoint

This viewpoint centres only on the present moment. It discards past and future contexts. For example, in a desert, only a glass of water matters, not one's bank balance. Or a person once blessed with children but now alone must live with their current reality. Rujusutra Naya values what is immediately functional and relevant.

Naigama Naya – The Generalized/Integrative Viewpoint

Naigama Naya integrates all three-time dimensions — past, present, and future. When someone says, "I am going to grind flour," the wheat (present), grinding process (future), and flour (result) are interconnected. We often refer to an empty juice bottle as a "juice bottle" due to its past function. This viewpoint allows practical functionality across time.

Samprata Naya – The Contextual / Linguistic Nuance Viewpoint

Samprata Naya emphasizes how linguistic elements like tense, tone, and gender affect meaning. For instance, "Ayodhya was" versus "Ayodhya is" can trigger vastly different mental images. It shows how our understanding is shaped by grammatical and contextual shifts in expression.

Samabhirudha Naya – The Semantic Nuance Viewpoint

This Naya explores synonyms and their contextual usage. Words like Netra, Aankh, Chakshu, Lochan all mean "eye," but their emotional or situational appropriateness varies. No two words are ever entirely synonymous; each carries unique connotations.

Evambhuta Naya – The Visual Connotation Viewpoint

Evambhuta Naya states that every word evokes a specific mental image. Say "school," and you visualize classrooms and children — not locked gates. Say "king," and you see a throne and court — not the king eating alone. This Naya highlights the imagination and symbolism that words naturally carry.

Conclusion

The seven Nayas offer powerful tools to interpret the world with nuance and sensitivity. By practicing these viewpoints, we improve our ability to analyze texts, interactions, and realities — leading to deeper understanding (Samyak Gyan) and spiritual advancement toward Moksha.

Simplified Definitions of the Seven Nayas (Viewpoints) in Jain Philosophy

Naya	Definition
Naigama	Perspectives that encompass all three tenses (past, present, and future), connect past and future events to the present, and use contextual expressions accordingly.
Samgraha	Perspectives inclined toward seeing similarities and unity among objects, focusing on the essence of oneness and aiming for refined expressions.

Vyavahara	Perspectives inclined toward observing differences among objects, emphasizing distinctions, and forming expressions grounded in conventional or practical usage.
Rujusutra	Perspectives focused solely on the present, considering what exists right now, what belongs to oneself, and what one currently possesses as the only relevant truths.
Samprata	Perspectives that explore how the meaning of identical words changes with variations in gender, tense, case, etc., and analyse these nuances.
Samabhirudha	Perspectives that delve into the subtle differences in meaning or connote-tion among synonyms, focusing on their precise and context-specific usage in language.
Evambhuta	Perspectives that analyse the mental images associated with words upon hearing or speaking to them and consider their ultimate significance or interpretations.

6

Understanding Nikshepa: The Layers of Meaning in a Word

Nikshepa refers to the philosophical process of examining the various meanings of a single word. It establishes the relationship between a word and its meanings — understanding not just what a word says, but all that it could possibly signify based on context.

Illustration: The Word "Indra"

Take the word Indra. It typically means the king of gods, but its usage spans across:

1. **Naam Nikshepa (Name Category)** – "Indra" as someone's name.
2. **Sthapana Nikshepa (Establishment Category)** – A written word 'Indra' or an idol symbolizing Indra.
3. **Dravya Nikshepa (Matter Category)** – A soul who was or will be Indra in another lifetime.
4. **Bhava Nikshepa (State/Emotion Category)** – When the soul actually embodies the essence of Indra.

The Four Main Types of Nikshepa

Nikshepa	Meaning & Example
Naam Nikshepa	Identifies something by its label or name. E.g., writing or speaking the word Indra or calling someone Indra.
Sthapana Nikshepa	Symbolic representation of something, with two subtypes: 1. Sadbhut Sthapana – Realistic models or depictions (e.g., statue of a Guru). 2. Asadbhut Sthapana – Abstract or imaginative symbols (e.g., footprints of the Guru).
Dravya Nikshepa	Refers to a being based on their past or future existence. E.g., a soul previously born as Indra, or destined to become Indra.
Bhava Nikshepa	The actual internal essence, the realized state. E.g., when a soul embodies the attributes of Indra.

Example Applications

Mangal (Auspicious)

- Naam: A person named Mangala
- Sthapana: Symbols like Swastika or Ashtamangal (Asadbhut)
- Dravya: A person or object that truly brings auspiciousness
- Bhava: The rise of virtue (Punya), fall of sin (Paap)

Mahavira

- Naam: Someone named Mahavira or the word itself
- Sadbhut Sthapana: A statue of Tirthankar Mahavira
- Asadbhut Sthapana: His footprints in Pavapuri
- Dravya: Mahavira in his past life as Marichi or now in Moksha
- Bhava: The life in which he attained complete self-realization

How to Apply Nikshepa in Scriptural Interpretation

When interpreting any scriptural sentence:

- Identify the possible meanings of each word.
- Contextually determine which Nikshepa (layer of meaning) applies.
- Arrive at the most accurate and meaningful interpretation.

7

The Five Contributing Factors Behind Every Action

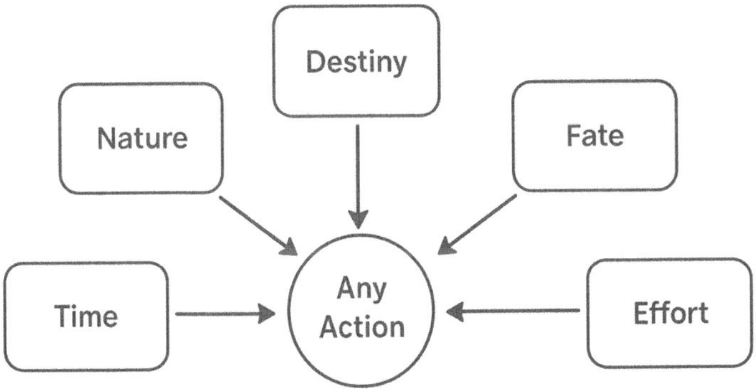

For any action (Karya) to manifest, **five factors** must come together:

- Kaal (Time)
- Swabhav (Nature)
- Prarabdh (Fate)
- Niyati (Destiny / Cosmic Arrangement)
- Purusharth (Effort)

1. Kaal (Time)

- Every action occurs at a designated moment, governed by time.

- A woman destined for motherhood will not bear a child at age 8 — the potential exists, but time must mature.
- Just as lentils require time to cook, events unfold only when their time is ripe.
- Kaal inherently brings transformation.

2. Swabhav (Nature)

- Refers to the intrinsic potential or characteristics of a being or object.
- Silk is smooth; lentils are cookable — this is their Swabhav.
- The essence of Tirthankartva (potential to become a Tirthankara) is embedded within the soul — it cannot be externally given, only developed.
- Swabhav is the root of Jeevadal — the potential of life.

3. Prarabdh (Fate)

- Prarabdh encompasses one's accumulated karmas — both Punya (virtue) and Paap (sin) — from past lives.
- It is deeply personal and individual.

Example:

- Mahavirswami's transition from Devananda's womb to Trishala's represents the fruition of Uchchgotra Karma and the end of Neechgotra Karma.
- Such karmic exchanges, seen in multiple lives, illustrate the working of Prarabdh.

4. Niyati (Cosmic Arrangement / Divine Order)

- Niyati is the supreme system that ensures karmic coordination across souls.
- It is not the same as Prarabdh. Prarabdh is individual; Niyati is universal.

It operates in two ways:

- **Coordinates Karma** – aligning multiple souls' karmas for a shared outcome.
- **Takes over where Karma ends** – e.g., deciding which soul will rise from Nigod after another attains Moksha.

Niyati transcends Karma Satta — the realm of karmic authority.

5. Purusharth (Effort)

- The only one among the five under our control.

- Even when the other four align, nothing manifests without Purusharth.
- Purusharth alone has the power to influence even destiny and alter cosmic arrangements, provided it becomes strong enough.
- Without it, all other factors remain dormant.

Interconnection and Functionality

- All five factors contribute equally — each about 20%.
- Yet depending on the situation, one may appear more dominant.

Example of Misplaced Attribution:

- We say: "Time was right" (emphasizing Kaal) or "It's his nature" (highlighting Swabhav).
- But without effort (Purusharth), neither time nor nature can bring results.

The Role of Niyati in Collective Karma

When multiple karmas need to align — as in the case of Mahavirswami's birth — Niyati acts as the invisible arranger.

It ensures that events unfold in perfect synchrony across individuals and timelines.

Example:

Rishabhadatta losing the opportunity to become a father of Mahavirswami and Siddharth Raja gaining it reflects not just Prarabdh but a higher orchestration – Niyati.

Special Scenarios

- When Karma is indistinct or inactive (e.g., Nigod souls, which are virtually identical), Niyati alone decides which soul rises.
- When Karma Satta ends, Niyati begins.

Application in the Spiritual Path

- Emergence from Nigod → Niyati
- Entry into Charam Pudgal Paravartan → Kaal
- Capacity for liberation (Bhavyatva) → Swabhav
- Favorable conditions for sadhana → Prarabdh
- Actual practice of spiritual pursuit → Purusharth

Together, these five comprise Tathabhavyatva – the timely, harmonious interplay of all five for spiritual evolution.

What Should We Focus On?

- While Tirthankaras can perceive and respect the system of Niyati through their omniscience, we cannot.
- Hence, our focus must be on **Purusharth**.
- By assessing our **Bhavyatva** (potential for liberation), we must put our full effort into spiritual progress — the only factor entirely in our hands.

Glossary of Key Jain Philosophical Terms

Term	Definition
Anekanta	Anekanta is the fundamental Jain philosophical principle that truth and reality are complex and can be viewed from multiple perspectives. No single statement can capture the full truth absolutely; instead, each perspective holds a partial truth depending on context, time, and viewpoint.
Anekantvad	The doctrine of pluralism which teaches that reality is complex and cannot be fully explained from a single viewpoint.
Anuyog	A method or approach to scriptural interpretation; includes four types—Dravyanuyog, Charananuyog, Dharmakathanuyog, and Ganitanuyog.
Bhavyatva	The inherent potential or capacity of a soul to attain liberation (Moksha).
Charam Pudgal Paravartan	The final transformation of karmic matter before achieving liberation (Moksha).

Term	Definition
Dhrauvya	Stability or constancy of the underlying substance across changing forms.
Dravya	Substance or matter; the base entity that possesses qualities (Guna) and undergoes forms (Paryaya).
Evambhuta Naya	A perspective based on the mental imagery or conceptual picture evoked by a word.
Guna	Inherent and unchanging qualities or properties of a substance.
Kevalgyan	Kevalgyan is the state of complete and perfect knowledge attained by a soul that has eradicated all obscuring karmas. A Kevalgyani perceives all truths, in all places, times, and modes, simultaneously and directly.
Naigama Naya	Viewpoint combining past, present, and future tenses; a general or goal-oriented perspective.
Naya	A particular viewpoint or perspective used to understand and express aspects of truth; Jain philosophy defines seven types of Nayas.

Term	Definition
Nigod	The lowest form of existence where souls are minimally active and bound in clusters; emergence from Nigod marks the beginning of spiritual evolution.
Nikshepa	The analysis of a word or concept through four dimensions: Name (Naam), Representation (Sthapana), Substance (Dravya), and State (Bhava).
Nimitt Karan	The instrumental cause or condition that helps the material cause manifest into a specific form.
Niyati	Cosmic arrangement or inevitability that governs the unfolding of events beyond personal karma.
Paryaya	The changing state or form of a substance over time; modifications that occur moment to moment.
Prarabdh	Fate or results of karmic actions from past lives.
Purusharth	Personal effort or willpower applied toward achieving goals, including spiritual progress.

Term	Definition
Rujusutra Naya	A perspective focused only on the present moment and its relevance.
Samabhirudha Naya	A viewpoint that differentiates synonyms based on their connotations and contextual appropriateness.
Samgraha Naya	The collective viewpoint that emphasizes commonality or unity.
Samprata Naya	A viewpoint considering how meaning changes with language variations like gender, tense, and case.
Saptabhangi	The sevenfold predication theory that presents different perspectives of truth, affirming, denying, and combining states.
Swabhav	The intrinsic nature or characteristic of a being or substance.
Syadvad	The doctrine of conditional or contextual predication — "in some respect it is, and in some respect it is not" — based on Anekantvad.

Term	Definition
Tathabhavyatva	The timely and appropriate activation of all five factors—Time, Nature, Destiny, Fate, and Effort—for any event or spiritual outcome to occur.
Upadan Dravya	The material cause or base substance from which something is formed.
Utpad	Origination or arising of a new state/form in a substance.
Vinash	Destruction or cessation of a previous state/form.
Vyavahara Naya	The practical viewpoint that emphasizes differences and distinctions.

Bibliography

Primary Author:

Trailokyamandan Vijay Maharaj – Author of the original discourses compiled and presented in this booklet.

Presenting Organization:

Mandan Parivar – For conceptualizing and presenting the 'A Ray of Hope' series and making this compilation accessible to a wider audience. A Ray of Hope Series (A10), Veer 2551 / A.D. 2025

Philosophical Sources and Influences:

- Agam Scriptures – Canonical Jain texts referenced implicitly throughout the discourse, especially in context to Anekanta, Syadvad, and Nayavad.
- *Sanmatitarka* by *Acharya Siddhasen Diwakar* – Foundational work on logic and the early structured explanation of Anekanta.
- *Nyayavatara, Batrisabatrisi* – Jain logical treatises attributed to *Acharya Siddhasen Diwakar*.
- *Devagama Stotra* – Contributions of *Acharya Samantabhadra* in refining Anekanta philosophy.

- Contributions by Jain scholars such as *Acharya Shri Haribhadrasuriji Maharaj*, *Kalikalsarvagna* Shri *Hemchandracharya*, *Upadhyay Yashovijayji*, *Bhatt Akalankadev*, and *Vidyanandswami*.

Key Concepts and Philosophical Frameworks:

- **Anekanta (Pluralism)** – The core subject of the text, explored through multiple discourses and analogies.
- **Syadvad and Nayavad** – Frameworks used to explain the expression and perspectives of truth.
- **Nikshepa and Panchakaran Samavay** – Classical philosophical structures drawn from Jain epistemology.

Illustrative Analogies Referenced:

- The Parable of the Blind Men and the Elephant.
- The Necklace of Principles (from *Sanmatitarka*).
- Hut and Light analogy for partial truth.
- Lock and Ten Keys metaphor.
- Honeybee analogy for spiritual receptivity.

A Final Word: Anekanta as a Way Forward

This humble effort, spread across more than two hundred pages, is not the end – but a beginning.

Anekanta is not just a philosophical lens; it is an invitation to live with deeper awareness, softer judgments, and expansive understanding. In a world increasingly defined by rigidity and conflict, this ancient Jain wisdom reminds us: truth is vast, layered, and dynamic. What we perceive is often just a fragment.

The practice of Anekanta begins not in temples or classrooms, but in daily conversations, disagreements, and quiet introspections. Each time we choose empathy over ego, patience over reaction, and curiosity over certainty – we honour the spirit of Anekanta.

Let these teachings continue to echo in your life beyond these pages. May your journey ahead be one of questioning, unfolding, and ultimately – liberation.

With reverence and hope,

A Ray of Hope